THE BEST
GENERATION
OF MUSLIMS

© 2024 Imam Ghazali Publishing, USA

No part of this publication may be reproduced, stored in a retrieval system, or transmitted in any form or by any means, electronic or otherwise, including photocopying, recording and internet without prior permission of the Imam Ghazali Publishing.

The views, information, or opinions expressed are solely those of the author(s) and do not necessarily represent those of Imam Ghazali Publishing.

Title: The Best Generation of Muslims
ISBN: 978-1-952306-51-8

Author: Imam Yusuf al-Nabahani
Translation: Ahmad Derrick Peat

Imam Ghazali Publishing
www.imamghazali.co
info@imamghazali.co

THE BEST GENERATION OF MUSLIMS

FORTY HADITH ON THE COMPANIONS OF THE MESSENGER ﷺ

COMPILED BY
Imam Yusuf al-Nabahani

TRANSLATION BY
Ahmad Derrick Peat

رضي الله عنهم

Table of Contents

Hadith One 3
Hadith Two 4
Hadith Three 5
Hadith Four 7
Hadith Five 8
Hadith Six 9
Hadith Seven 10
Hadith Eight 12
Hadith Nine 13
Hadith Ten 15
Hadith Eleven 16
Hadith Twelve 18
Hadith Thirteen 20
Hadith Fourteen 22
Hadith Fifteen 23
Hadith Sixteen 24
Hadith Seventeen 26
Hadith Eighteen 28
Hadith Nineteen 29
Hadith Twenty 30
Hadith Twenty-One 31
Hadith Twenty-Two 33
Hadith Twenty-Three 35
Hadith Twenty-Four 36
Hadith Twenty-Five 37
Hadith Twenty-Six 38

Hadith Twenty-Seven 39
Hadith Twenty-Eight 40
Hadith Twenty-Nine 41
Hadith Thirty 44
Hadith Thirty-One 46
Hadith Thirty-Two 47
Hadith Thirty-Three 48
Hadith Thirty-Four 50
Hadith Thirty-Five 51
Hadith Thirty-Six 52
Hadith Thirty-Seven 54
Hadith Thirty-Eight 55
Hadith Thirty-Nine 57
Hadith Forty... 58
Conclusion: On the Virtues of the Companions altogether as a Class by Themselves 59

Shaykh Yusuf al-Nabahani

By Shaykh GF Haddad

His Background

Imam Yusuf al-Nabahani wrote of himself in his first published book, al-Sharaf al-Mu'abbad li Ali Muhammad a (1891 CE/1309 AH), and in Asbab al-Ta'lif lil-'Abdi al-Da'if, and also in Jami' Karamat al-Awliya' (both in 1911 CE/1329 AH):

"I am the faqir Yusuf ibn Isma'il ibn Yusuf ibn Isma'il ibn Muhammad Nasir al-Din al-Nabahani. We go back to the Banu Nabhan, an Arab desert folk who settled of old in the town of Ijzim, north of the Holy sites in the land of Palestine, presently part of the district of Hayfah in 'Akka, province of Beirut. I was born in Ijzim in 1849 CE (1265 AH) approximately.

I read the Qur'an with my Master and father, the righteous Shaykh and meticulous memorizer of the Book of Allah, Shaykh Isma'il al-Nabahani who is now (in 1891 CE) past eighty, in full possession of his senses, of strong build and excellent health, and who spends most of his time in works of obedience.

My father's daily devotion in every twenty-four hours was one third of the Qur'an, then he would complete the Qur'an three times every week. The praise for this belongs to Allah!

'Say: In the bounty of Allah and in His mercy: therein let them rejoice. It is better than what they hoard.'" (10:58)

His Studies and Teachers

"Then he sent me - Allah ﷺ save him and thank him on my behalf! - to Cairo to study. I entered the Mosque of al-Azhar on Saturday in early Muharram of the year 1283 AH (16 May 1866 CE) and resided there until Rajab of 1289 AH (October 1872 CE). During that time, I learnt all that Allah ﷻ destined for me to learn of the sciences of the shari'ah and its preparatory disciplines at the hands of the accomplished teachers and major established masters of the time, any one of whom, if he were found in a place, would be the leader of its people to the gardens of Paradise and would meet their requirements in all of the sciences - the spoken and the rational.

One of them, or rather their peerless leader was the accomplished, erudite teacher, the refuge of meticulous understanding, the Shaykh of all shaykhs, Teacher of all teachers, Sayyidi al-Shaykh Ibrahim al-Saqqa al-Shafi'i who died in 1298 AH aged around ninety years. He spent his entire blessed long life reading lessons until most of the scholars ('ulama') of our time became his students, either directly, or through an intermediary.

I attended his classes –may Allah ﷻ have mercy on him! - for three years and learnt from him the two commentaries, al-Tahrir and al-Manhaj, of Shaykh al-Islam Zakariya al-Ansari together with their marginalia by al-Sharqawi and al-Bujayrimi respectively.

Other Teachers Include:

The venerable erudite scholar, Sayyidi al-Shaykh al-Sayyid Muhammad al-Damanhuri al-Shafi'i who died in 1286 AH aged around ninety years.

The erudite Scholar Sayyidi al-Shaykh Ibrahim al-Zurru al-Khalili al-Shafi'i who died in 1287 AH aged around seventy.

The erudite Scholar Sayyidi al-Shaykh Ahmad al-Ajhuri al-Darir al-Shafi'i who died in 1293 AH aged around sixty.

The erudite Scholar Sayyidi al-Shaykh Hasan al-'Adawi al-Maliki who died in 1298 AH aged around eighty.

The erudite Scholar Sayyidi al-Shaykh al-Sayyid 'Abd al-Hadi Naja al-Abyari who died in 1305 AH aged just over seventy years.

Shaykh Shams al-Din Muhammad al-Anbabi al-Shafi'i the Master of al-Azhar Mosque, who died in 1313 AH.

Shaykh 'Abd al-Rahman al-Sharbini al-Shafi'i the Master of al-Azhar Mosque, who died in 1326 AH.

Shaykh 'Abd al-Qadir al-Rafi'i al-Hanafi al-Tarabulsi the Master of the Damascenes' Porch (Ruwaq al-Shawamm) in al-Azhar Mosque, who died in 1323 AH.

Shaykh Yusuf al-Barqawi al-Hanbali the Master of the Hanbalis' Porch in al-Azhar Mosque.

His Teaching and Positions

"[After graduating and returning home to Ijzim] I began to hold a number of religious courses in 'Akka and my home town of Ijzim. Then I travelled frequently to Beirut, then Damascus where I met the eminent 'Ulama'. The chief among them was the Jurist of Damascus at the time, our Master the erudite Imam, al-Sayyid al-Sharif Mahmud Effendi Hamza – may Allah have mercy on him - with whom I learnt the beginning of al-Bukhari's Sahih, after which he gave me a general certificate comprising the rest of the Sahih, as well as all his other narrations and his own works. He wrote this long certificate in his superb style and handsome handwriting.

Then I headed to Constantinople twice and worked there for several years. I edited the periodical al-Jawa'ib until it folded. I also proofread the Arabic books that came out of its press. My monthly salary there was ten Liras for editing and proofreading. I worked on this for about two or three hours [daily] and did it on the insistent request of the paper's owner, Ahmad Effendi Faris. He considered me his greatest blessing and showed great sadness at seeing me leave for my new position with the government [as a judge]. He offered me to work as his partner or a raise, but I refused.

I left Constantinople for the first time, for Iraq. I went to the district of Kawi Sanjaq in the province of Mosul. Then I returned to Constantinople. I left for a second time in 1300 AH when I was appointed head judge of al-Jaza' court in al-Ladhiqiya on the Syro-Palestinian sea-shore. After living there for five years the Dawla – may Allah grant her victory - transferred me to the head judgeship of the court of al-Quds al-Sharif. This took place through those at whose hands Allah decreed goodness for me, without request nor prior knowledge on my part. Then, after less than a year; eight months to be precise, they promoted me, without request nor prior knowledge on my part, to the chief judgeship of the Beirut Court of Justice. This was in 1305 AH (1888 CE)."

A Selection of His Works

Ahsan al-Wasa'il fi Nazmi Asma'i al-Nabiyi al-Kamil (The Best Means in Versifying the Names of the Perfect Prophet ﷺ), in three hundred verses, in print. The Qadi wrote a brief history on the compilations of the Prophetic Names in his introduction to his commentary on al-Jazuli's Dala'il titled al-Dalalat al-Wadihat in which he mentioned various recensions to date:

Al-Qadi 'Iyad's superlative masterpiece al-Shifa' Al-Fakihani's al-Fajr al-Munir

Abu 'Imran al-Zanati's compendium (201 names)

Al-Jazuli's devotional masterpiece Dala'il al-Khayrat in which he relied on al-Zanati's work

Al-Suyuti's al-Hada'iq fi Asma'i Khayr al-Khala'iq (300+ names)

Al-Suyuti's al-Riyad al-Aniqa fi Asma'i Khayr al-Khaliqah listing sources for the Hada'iq

Al-Suyuti's al-Bahjat al-Saniya (500 names)

Al-Sakhawi's al-Qawl al-Badi' fi al-Salat 'alá al-Habib al-Shafi' (450 names)

Al-Qastalani's al-Mawahib al-Laduniya in which he relied on al-Sakhawi's work

Al-Zurqani's Sharh al-Mawahib (800+ names)

Al-Nabahani's Ahsan al-Wasa'il in verse and al-Asma' fi ma li-Rasulillahi min al-Asma' in prose (830 names)

A trilingual recension was recently published by Shaykh Anis Ludhianvi

Al-Arba'ina Arba'in min Ahadith Sayyid al-Mursalin (Forty Times Forty Narrations from the Master of Messengers).

Jami' Karamat al-Awliya' (Compendium of the Miraculous Gifts of Allah's Friends) in two volumes. This was later reprinted in Beirut by al-Maktaba al-Thaqafiya, in 1991. It is an encyclopedia on the miracles of Muslim Saints.

Mithal al-Na'l al-Sharif (The Image of the Noble Sandals [of the Prophet ﷺ]), in print.

The major Indian Hanafi Scholar Mawlana Ashraf 'Ali al-Thanwi titled a chapter Nayl al-Shifa' bi-Na'l al-Mustafá (Attaining a Remedy through the Sandals of the Chosen One ﷺ) in his book Zad al-Sa'id (Provision for the Fortunate). The Shaykh of our Shuyukh and Muhaddith of India, Shaykh Muhammad Zakariya Kandhlawi ﷺ said in his translation of Imam al-Tirmidhi's foundational work al-Shama'il al-Nabawiyah wa al-Khasa'il al-Mustafawiyah (The Prophetic Traits and Muhammadan Features):

Mawlana Ashraf 'Ali Thanwi Sahib has written in his book Zad al-Sa'id a detailed treatise on the blessings and virtues of the Messenger's shoes. Those interested in it should read the book. In short, it may be said that it [the Prophet's sandal] has countless qualities.

The 'Ulama' have had experiences from time to time; One is blessed [through it] with seeing Allah's Messenger ﷺ in their dreams, they are granted safety from their oppressors and every heartfelt desire is attained. Every objective is fulfilled by its tawassul. The method of tawassul [using a means] is also mentioned therein.

1. Al-Tahdhir min Ittikhadh al-Suwar wa al-Taswir (The Warning against taking Photographs and Photography).

2. Wasa'il al-Wusul ila Shama'il al-Rasul ﷺ (The Means to the Characteristics of the Messenger ﷺ), a summary on Imam al-Tirmidhi's Shama'il.

His Death

After al-Nabahani ﷺ retired, he turned entirely to writing and worshipping. He travelled to al-Madinah al-Munawwarah and lived in the noble city for a period. Then he returned to Beirut where he passed on to the mercy of His Lord in the beginning of the month of Ramadan 1350 AH (1932 CE).

THE BEST GENERATION OF MUSLIMS

FORTY HADITH ON THE VIRTUES OF THE COMPANIONS

COMPILED BY
Imam Yusuf al-Nabahani

TRANSLATION BY
Ahmad Derrick Peat

Author's Introduction

بسم الله الرحمن الرحيم

In the name of Allah, the Beneficent, the Most Merciful

الحَمْدُ لله رَبِّ العَالَمِيْنَ, وَالصَّلَاةُ وَالسَّلَامُ عَلَى سَيِّدِنَا مُحَمَّدٍ سَيِّدِ المُرْسَلِيْنَ, وَعَلَى آلِهِ وَصَحْبِهِ أَجْمَعِيْنَ. أَمَّا بَعْدُ, فَهَذِهِ أَرْبَعُوْنَ حَدِيْثاً فِيْ فَضْلِ أَرْبَعِيْنَ مِنَ الصَّحَابَةِ رَضِيَ اللهُ عَنْهُمْ, وَجَعَلْتُ لَهَا خَاتِمَةً فِيْ فَضْلِ الصَّحَابَةِ مُطْلَقاً رَضِيَ اللهُ عَنْهُمْ أَجْمَعِيْنَ.

All praise is due to Allah, the Lord of the worlds. May Allah bless and grant peace to our master, Muhammad, to his family and to all his companions, amin.

The following is compilation of 40 hadiths extolling the qualities, merits and virtues of certain companions (may Allah be pleased with them, and may He grant them contentment). I have appended this collection with a section dedicated to praising all of the companions in general. May Allah be pleased with all of them.

HADITH ONE

١- فَضْلُ أَبِي بَكْرٍ رَضِيَ اللهُ عَنْهُ: أَخْرَجَ الشَّيْخَانِ عَنْ أَبِي سَعِيدٍ الْخُدْرِيِّ رَضِيَ اللهُ عَنْهُ عَنِ النَّبِيِّ صَلَّى اللهُ عَلَيْهِ وَسَلَّمَ قَالَ: «إِنَّ مِنْ أَمَنِّ النَّاسِ عَلَيَّ فِي صُحْبَتِهِ وَمَالِهِ أَبَا بَكْرٍ, وَلَوْ كُنْتُ مُتَّخِذاً خَلِيلاً لَاتَّخَذْتُ أَبَا بَكْرٍ خَلِيلاً, وَلَكِنْ أُخُوَّةُ الْإِسْلَامِ وَمَوَدَّتُهُ, لَا تَبْقَيَنَّ فِي الْمَسْجِدِ خَوْخَةٌ إِلَّا خَوْخَةُ أَبِي بَكْرٍ». وَفِي رِوَايَةٍ: «لَوْ كُنْتُ مُتَّخِذاً خَلِيلاً غَيْرَ رَبِّي لَاتَّخَذْتُ أَبَا بَكْرٍ خَلِيلاً».⁽¹⁾

Concerning the excellence of Abu Bakr (may Allah be pleased with him, and may He grant him contentment), the two Shaykhs[2] narrate that Abu Saʿid al-Khudri (may Allah be pleased with him, and may He grant him contentment) reported that the Prophet (may Allah bless him, and may He grant him contentment) said, "Among the leading people who put their trust in me and supported me with their comradery, friendship and wealth is Abu Bakr; if I were to take a close confidant, I would take Abu Bakr as my confidant, but in the place of such friendship is the general love and fraternity enjoined by Islam. So from this moment on let there remain no wicket *[khukha]* in my mosque except that of Abu Bakr."[3]

---

(١) أخرجه البخاري (٣٤٠٥), والبغوي في شرح السنة (٣٧٣١).

(2) In the terminology of the scholars of hadith, "the two Shaykhs" is designated to mean al-Bukhari and Muslim (may Allah be pleased with them, and may He grant them contentment).

(3) Translator's note: Some scholars, of hadith , such as ibn Hibban utilized this narration to affirm Abu Bakr's suitability to be the first caliph of the Muslims.

HADITH TWO

٢- فَضْلُ عُمَرَ رَضِيَ اللهُ عَنْهُ: أَخْرَجَ الشَّيْخَانِ عَنْ أَبِي سَعِيدٍ رَضِيَ اللهُ عَنْهُ قَالَ: قَالَ رَسُوْلُ اللهِ صَلَّى اللهُ عَلَيْهِ وَسَلَّمَ: «بَيْنَا أَنَا نَائِمٌ، رَأَيْتُ النَّاسَ يُعْرَضُوْنَ عَلَيَّ وَعَلَيْهِمْ قُمُصٌ، مِنْهَا مَا يَبْلُغُ الثُّدِيَّ، وَمِنْهَا مَا دُوْنَ ذَلِكَ، وعُرِضَ عَلَيَّ عُمَرُ بْنُ الْخَطَّابِ وَعَلَيْهِ قَمِيْصٌ يَجُرُّهُ» قَالُوا: فَمَا أَوَّلْتَ ذَلِكَ يَا رَسُوْلَ اللهِ؟ قَالَ: «الدِّيْنَ» (٤).

On the excellence of 'Umar (may Allah be pleased with him, and may He grant him contentment), the two Shaykhs also narrated that Abu Sa'id al-Khudri (may Allah be pleased with him, and may He grant him contentment) reported that Allah's Emissary (may Allah bless him, and may He grant him peace) said, "I have seen mankind in a dream, and they were being presented to me while they were wearing upper body garments; some of these garments stretched down covering people's chests, while other garments reached below that. 'Umar ibn al-Khattab (may Allah be pleased with him, and may He grant him contentment) was then presented to me, and he was wearing a short that stretched so far down that he was forced to drag it behind him." The companions asked the Prophet (may Allah bless him, and may He grant him peace), "What is your interpretation for this vision, oh Emissary of Allah?" "Piety," responded the Prophet (may Allah bless him, and may He grant him peace).

---

(٤) أخرجه البخاري (٢٣) ومسلم (٢٣٩٢).

HADITH THREE

٣- فَضْلُ عُثْمَانَ رَضِيَ اللهُ عَنْهُ: أَخْرَجَ مُسْلِمٌ عَنْ عَائِشَةَ رَضِيَ اللهُ عَنْهَا قَالَتْ: «كَانَ رَسُولُ اللهِ صَلَّى اللهُ عَلَيْهِ وَسَلَّمَ مُضْطَجِعًا فِي بَيْتِهِ, كَاشِفًا عَنْ فَخِذَيْهِ, أَوْ سَاقَيْهِ, فَاسْتَأْذَنَ أَبُو بَكْرٍ, فَأَذِنَ لَهُ, وَهُوَ عَلَى تِلْكَ الحَالِ, فَتَحَدَّثَا, ثُمَّ اسْتَأْذَنَ عُمَرُ, فَأَذِنَ لَهُ وَهُوَ كَذَلِكَ, فَتَحَدَّثَا, ثُمَّ اسْتَأْذَنَ عُثْمَانُ, فَجَلَسَ رَسُولُ اللهِ صَلَّى اللهُ عَلَيْهِ وَسَلَّمَ وَسَوَّى ثِيَابَهُ, فَلَمَّا خَرَجَ قَالَتْ عَائِشَةُ: دَخَلَ أَبُو بَكْرٍ فَلَمْ تَهْتَشَّ لَهُ وَلَمْ تُبَالِهِ, ثُمَّ دَخَلَ عُمَرُ فَلَمْ تَهْتَشَّ لَهُ وَلَمْ تُبَالِهِ, ثُمَّ دَخَلَ عُثْمَانُ فَجَلَسْتَ وَسَوَّيْتَ ثِيَابَكَ, فَقَالَ: أَلَا أَسْتَحِي مِنْ رَجُلٍ تَسْتَحِي مِنْهُ الْمَلَائِكَةُ» (٥).

Concerning the stature of 'Uthman (may Allah be pleased with him, and may He grant him contentment), Imam Muslim recorded that 'Aisha (may Allah be pleased with her, and may He grant her contentment) narrated, "The Messenger of Allah (may Allah bless him, and may He grant him peace) was once reclining inside his room with his thighs and shins uncovered when Abu Bakr sought permission to enter; the Prophet (may Allah bless him, and may He grant him peace) gave him permission while remaining as he was before Abu Bakr entered. They spoke for a while until 'Umar sought permission to enter, and the Prophet (may Allah bless him, and may He grant him peace) permitted him while remaining with his thighs and shins uncovered. They conversed with each other until 'Uthman

---

(٥) أخرجه مسلم (٦٣٦٢).

sought permission to enter upon which the Prophet (may Allah bless him, and may He grant him peace) got up and put on his garments. Later on, 'Aisha asked the the Prophet (may Allah bless him, and may He grant him peace), 'When Abu Bakr entered you did not ready yourself, and it was apparent that you were unruffled by his arrival. Then 'Umar came and you did not change your appearance for meeting him, and you were unruffled by his arrival. But then, when 'Uthman sought permission to enter, you sat up covering and preparing yourself?' 'Shall I not be shy in the presence of a man who the angels are shy in front of?' the Prophet (may Allah bless him, and may He grant him peace) responded."

HADITH FOUR

٤- فَضْلُ عَلِيٍّ رَضِيَ اللهُ عَنْهُ: أَخْرَجَ الشَّيْخَانِ عَنْ سَعْدِ بْنِ أَبِي وَقَّاصٍ رَضِيَ اللهُ عَنْهُ قَالَ: قَالَ رَسُولُ اللهِ صَلَّى اللهُ عَلَيْهِ وَسَلَّمَ لِعَلِيٍّ: «أَنْتَ مِنِّي بِمَنْزِلَةِ هَارُونَ مِنْ مُوسَى، إِلَّا أَنَّهُ لَا نَبِيَّ بَعْدِي» (٦).

Concerning the excellence of 'Ali (may Allah be pleased with him, and may He grant him contentment), the two Shaykhs recorded that Sa'd ibn Abi Waqqas (may Allah be pleased with him, and may He grant him contentment) narrated that the Messenger of Allah (may Allah bless him, and may He grant him peace) once said to 'Ali, "Your position in regards to me is like the position of Harun in regards to Musa, except it is the case that there is no prophet after me."

---

(٦) أخرجه البخاري (٤٤١٦)، ومسلم (٦٣٧١).

HADITH FIVE

٥- فَضْلُ الحَسَنِ رَضِيَ اللهُ عَنْهُ: أَخْرَجَ الشَّيْخَانِ عَنِ البَرَاءِ بْنِ عَازِبٍ رَضِيَ اللهُ عَنْهُ قَالَ: رَأَيْتُ النَّبِيَّ صَلَّى اللهُ عَلَيْهِ وَسَلَّمَ حَمَلَ الحَسَنَ عَلَى عَاتِقِهِ, وَقَالَ: «اللَّهُمَّ إِنِّي أُحِبُّهُ فَأَحِبَّهُ». وَزَادَ ابْنُ عَسَاكِرَ: «وَأَحِبَّ مَنْ يُحِبُّهُ» (٧).

On the excellence of al-Hasan ibn 'Ali (may Allah be pleased with them both, and may He grant them contentment), the two Shaykhs recorded that al-Bara' ibn 'Azib (may Allah be pleased with him, and may He grant him contentment) said, "I once saw the Prophet (may Allah bless him, and may He grant him peace) carrying Hasan on his shoulders and he supplicated, 'Oh Allah! I do indeed love him, so show him Your love.'" Other hadith compilers such as ibn 'Asakir narrated a version of this event with the addition of, "…and show love to those who show him love."

---

(٧) أخرجه البخاري (٥٨٨٤), ومسلم (٦٤٠٩).

HADITH SIX

٦- فَضْلُ الْحُسَيْنِ رَضِيَ اللهُ عَنْهُ: أَخْرَجَ التِّرْمِذِيُّ عَنْ يَعْلَى بْنِ أُمَيَّةَ قَالَ: قَالَ رَسُولُ اللهِ صَلَّى اللهُ عَلَيْهِ وَسَلَّمَ: «حُسَيْنٌ مِنِّي وَأَنَا مِنْ حُسَيْنٍ، أَحَبَّ اللَّهُ مَنْ أَحَبَّ حُسَيْنًا، حُسَيْنٌ سِبْطٌ مِنَ الأَسْبَاطِ».(٨)

Imam at-Tirmithi reported concerning the excellence of al-Husayn (may Allah be pleased with him, and may He grant him contentment) that Ya'la ibn Umayya (may Allah be pleased with him, and may He grant him contentment) narrated that the Messenger of Allah (may Allah bless him, and may He grant him peace) said, "Husayn is from me, and I am from him. May Allah love whoever loves Husayn. Husayn is a slendid heir among the honored progeny."

---

(٨) أخرجه الترمذي (٣٧٧٥).

HADITH SEVEN

٧- فَضْلُ السَّيِّدَةِ فَاطِمَةَ الزَّهْرَاءِ رَضِيَ اللهُ عَنْهَا: أَخْرَجَ الشَّيْخَانِ عَنْ عَائِشَةَ رَضِيَ اللهُ عَنْهَا قَالَتْ: كُنَّا أَزْوَاجَ النَّبِيِّ صَلَّى اللهُ عَلَيْهِ وَسَلَّمَ عِنْدَهُ، فَأَقْبَلَتْ فَاطِمَةُ مَا تَخْفَى مِشْيَتُهَا مِنْ مِشْيَةِ رَسُولِ اللهِ صَلَّى اللهُ عَلَيْهِ وَسَلَّمَ، فَلَمَّا رَآهَا قَالَ: «مَرْحَبًا بِابْنَتِي», ثُمَّ أَجْلَسَهَا، ثُمَّ سَارَّهَا، فَبَكَتْ بُكَاءً شَدِيدًا، فَلَمَّا رَأَى حُزْنَهَا سَارَّهَا الثَّانِيَةَ، فَإِذَا هِيَ تَضْحَكُ، فَلَمَّا قَامَ رَسُولُ اللهِ صَلَّى اللهُ عَلَيْهِ وَسَلَّمَ سَأَلْتُهَا: عَمَّ سَارَّكِ؟ قَالَتْ: مَا كُنْتُ لِأُفْشِيَ عَلَى رَسُولِ اللهِ صَلَّى اللهُ عَلَيْهِ وَسَلَّمَ سِرَّهُ، فَلَمَّا تُوُفِّيَ، قُلْتُ: عَزَمْتُ عَلَيْكِ بِمَا لِي عَلَيْكِ مِنَ الْحَقِّ لَمَا أَخْبَرْتِنِي، قَالَتْ: أَمَّا الآنَ فَنَعَمْ، أَمَّا حِينَ سَارَّنِي فِي الأَمْرِ الأَوَّلِ، فَإِنَّهُ أَخْبَرَنِي: «أَنَّ جِبْرِيلَ كَانَ يُعَارِضُنِي الْقُرْآنَ كُلَّ سَنَةٍ مَرَّةً، وَإِنَّهُ قَدْ عَارَضَنِي بِهِ العَامَ مَرَّتَيْنِ، وَلاَ أَرَى الأَجَلَ إِلَّا قَدِ اقْتَرَبَ، فَاتَّقِي اللهَ وَاصْبِرِي، فَإِنِّي نِعْمَ السَّلَفُ أَنَا لَكِ» فَبَكَيْتُ، فَلَمَّا رَأَى جَزَعِي سَارَّنِي الثَّانِيَةَ، قَالَ: «يَا فَاطِمَةُ، أَلاَ تَرْضَيْنَ أَنْ تَكُونِي سَيِّدَةَ نِسَاءِ هَذِهِ الأُمَّةِ أَوْ نِسَاءِ المُؤْمِنِينَ» (٩).

Concerning the merits of Fatima az-Zahra' (may Allah be pleased with her, and may He grant her contentment), the two Shaykhs quoted 'Aisha (may Allah be pleased with her, and may He grant her contentment) as having said, "We, the wives of the Prophet (may Allah bless him, and may He grant him peace), were once in his presence when we recognized that Fatima was approaching because her

---

(٩) أخرجه البخاري (٣٤٢٦)، ومسلم (٢٤٥٠).

manner of walking was similar to that of the Prophet (may Allah bless him, and may He grant him peace). When he saw her, he said, 'My daughter! Welcome!' As he gave her a seat and greeted her further, she began crying profusely. He then continued speaking with her until she began to laugh. After the Messenger of Allah (may Allah bless him, and may He grant him peace) left the room, I asked Fatima, 'Why were you crying and then laughing so suddenly?' 'I am not one to reveal the Messenger's secret,' she responded. Some time later, after the Prophet (may Allah bless him, and may He grant him peace) had passed away, I asked her again, 'You really must tell me now; it is my right upon you that you tell me about what you refused to tell me before. What was it?' Fatima (may Allah be pleased with her, and He grant her contentment) responded, 'It would be my pleasure to tell you now what I could not reveal to you before. I came to see the Prophet that day, and as I sat down, he said, "It has been the case that Jibril tests my memorization of the Qur'an once every year, but this year he has come to me twice, and I can tell that this really means that my time of passing has come near; so hold firm to faith in Allah, and be patient. And it will be the case that my passing will precede yours only by a little." When the Prophet (may Allah bless him, and may He grant him peace) saw my anguish, he cheered me up saying, "Oh Fatima, does it not please you that you will become the noble empress amongst the people of paradise (or)¹⁰ of the believing women?"'"

---

(10) Translator's note: The "or" signifies that in the Arabic text the narrator of the hadith was not sure of the exact original wording of the Prophet's statement.

HADITH EIGHT

٨- فَضْلُ السَّيِّدَةِ خَدِيجَةَ أُمِّ الْمُؤْمِنِينَ رَضِيَ اللهُ عَنْهَا: أَخْرَجَ الْبُخَارِيُّ وَمُسْلِمٌ عَنْ عَلِيٍّ رَضِيَ اللهُ عَنْهُ قَالَ: سَمِعْتُ رَسُولَ اللهِ صَلَّى اللهُ عَلَيْهِ وَسَلَّمَ يَقُولُ: «خَيْرُ نِسَائِهَا مَرْيَمُ بِنْتُ عِمْرَانَ، وَخَيْرُ نِسَائِهَا خَدِيجَةُ بِنْتُ خُوَيْلِدٍ». وَفِي رِوَايَةٍ قَالَ أَبُو كُرَيْبٍ: وَأَشَارَ وَكِيعٌ -يَعْنِي: رَاوِيَ الْحَدِيثِ- إِلَى السَّمَاءِ وَالأَرْضِ (١١).

On the merit of the Honorable Khadija, the mother of the believers, Imams al-Bukhari and Muslim reported that 'Ali (may Allah be pleased with him, and may He grant him contentment) said, "I heard the Prophet (may Allah bless him, and may He grant him peace) say, 'The best of its[12] women are Maryam bint 'Imran and the best of its women are Khadija bint Khuwaylid.'" There is another narration in which Abu Kurayb explains the statement of the Prophet further by pointing to the heaven and the earth when mentioning "it."

---

(١١) أخرجه البخاري (٣٨١٥)، ومسلم (٢٤٣٠).

(12) "It" is a reference to all creation or all that is in the heavens and the earth.

HADITH NINE

٩- فَضْلُ السَّيِّدَةِ عَائِشَةَ أُمِّ المُؤْمِنِينَ رَضِيَ اللهُ عَنْهَا: أَخْرَجَ البُخَارِيُّ وَمُسْلِمٌ عَنْ عَائِشَةَ رَضِيَ اللهُ عَنْهَا قَالَتْ: إِنَّ النَّاسَ كَانُوا يَتَحَرَّوْنَ بِهَدَايَاهُمْ يَوْمَ عَائِشَةَ، يَبْتَغُونَ بِذَلِكَ مَرْضَاةَ رَسُولِ اللهِ صَلَّى اللهُ عَلَيْهِ وَسَلَّمَ(١٣).

وَقَالَتْ: إِنَّ نِسَاءَ رَسُولِ اللهِ صَلَّى اللهُ عَلَيْهِ وَسَلَّمَ كُنَّ حِزْبَيْنِ، فَحِزْبٌ فِيهِ عَائِشَةُ وَحَفْصَةُ وَصَفِيَّةُ وَسَوْدَةُ، وَالحِزْبُ الآخَرُ أُمُّ سَلَمَةَ وَسَائِرُ نِسَاءِ رَسُولِ اللهِ صَلَّى اللهُ عَلَيْهِ وَسَلَّمَ، فَكَلَّمَ حِزْبُ أُمِّ سَلَمَةَ فَقُلْنَ لَهَا: كَلِّمِي رَسُولَ اللهِ صَلَّى اللهُ عَلَيْهِ وَسَلَّمَ يُكَلِّمِ النَّاسَ، فَيَقُولُ: مَنْ أَرَادَ أَنْ يُهْدِيَ إِلَى رَسُولِ اللهِ صَلَّى اللهُ عَلَيْهِ وَسَلَّمَ فَلْيُهْدِ إِلَيْهِ حَيْثُ كَانَ، فَكَلَّمَتْهُ, فَقَالَ لَهَا: «لَا تُؤْذِينِي فِي عَائِشَةَ، فَإِنَّ الوَحْيَ لَمْ يَأْتِنِي وَأَنَا فِي ثَوْبِ امْرَأَةٍ إِلَّا عَائِشَةَ»، قَالَتْ: أَتُوبُ إِلَى اللهِ مِنْ أَذَاكَ يَا رَسُولَ اللهِ، ثُمَّ إِنَّهُنَّ دَعَوْنَ فَاطِمَةَ، فَأَرْسَلْنَهَا إِلَى رَسُولِ اللهِ صَلَّى اللهُ عَلَيْهِ وَسَلَّمَ فَكَلَّمَتْهُ, فَقَالَ: «يَا بُنَيَّةُ أَلَا تُحِبِّينَ مَا أُحِبُّ؟» قَالَتْ: بَلَى، قَالَ: «فَأَحِبِّي هَذِهِ»(١٤).

Concerning the stature of 'Aisha (may Allah be pleased with her, and He grant her contentment), Imams al-Bukhari and Muslim record that 'Aisha once narrated, "It was the case that the Muslims would bring gifts to the Messenger of Allah (may Allah bless him, and may He grant him peace) when it was 'Aisha's day to spend time with the Prophet (may Allah bless him, and may He grant him peace); they did this

---

(١٣) أخرجه البخاري (٢٥٨١)، ومسلم (٢٤٤١).

(١٤) أخرجه مسلم (٢٤٤٢).

seeking the good graces of Allah's Messenger (may Allah bless him, and may He grant him peace)." 'Aisha (may Allah be pleased with her, and may He grant her contentment) also added, "Further, the wives of the Prophet (may Allah bless him, and may He grant him peace) were divided into two groups; one group included 'Aisha, Hafsa, Safiyya and Sawda, and the other group included Umm Salama and the rest of the wives of the Messenger of Allah (may Allah bless him, and may He grant him peace). On an occasion, one of the members of Umm Salama's group spoke to Umm Salama and told her, 'Go and speak to Allah's Messenger (may Allah bless him, and may He grant him peace); tell him that he should tell the people to bring gifts on all the days, so Umm Salama spoke to him, but the Prophet swiftly responded, 'Do not disturb me with such statements against 'Aisha; revelation has never descended upon me when I was in close confines of any woman except 'Aisha (may Allah be pleased with her, and may He grant her contentment).' Umm Salama then said, 'I repent to Allah for annoying you, oh Messenger of Allah.' They then sought the assistance of Fatima (may Allah be pleased with her, and may He grant her contentment) sending her to intercede for them in front of Allah's Messenger (may Allah bless him, and may He grant him peace). As Fatima spoke to him, he said, 'Oh my daughter, do you not love what I love?' 'Of course I do,' responded Fatima. 'Then have love for her,' said the Prophet (may Allah bless him, and may He grant him peace)."

HADITH TEN

١٠- فَضْلُ زَيْدِ بْنِ حَارِثَةَ رَضِيَ اللهُ عَنْهُ: أَخْرَجَ ابْنُ عَسَاكِرَ عَنْ عَلِيٍّ رَضِيَ اللهُ عَنْهُ قَالَ: أَسْلَمَ زَيْدُ ابْنُ حَارِثَةَ مَوْلَى رَسُوْلِ اللهِ صَلَّى اللهُ عَلَيْهِ وَسَلَّمَ فَكَانَ أَوَّلَ ذَكَرٍ أَسْلَمَ وَصَلَّى (١٥).

وَأَخْرَجَ ابْنُ أَبِي شَيْبَةَ عَنْ عَبْدِ اللهِ بْنِ عُمَرَ رَضِيَ اللهُ عَنْهُمَا قَالَ: مَا كُنَّا نَدْعُوْ زَيْدَ بْنَ حَارِثَةَ إِلَّا زَيْدَ ابْنَ مُحَمَّدٍ حَتَّى نَزَلَ الْقُرْآنُ {ادْعُوهُمْ لِآبَائِهِمْ} (١٦).

Concerning the virtue of Zayd ibn Haritha (may Allah be pleased with him, and may He grant him contentment), ibn 'Asakir recorded that 'Ali (may Allah be pleased with him, and may He grant him contentment) said, "Zayd ibn Haritha, who was a client[17] of Allah's Messenger, accepted Islam; and he was, therefore, the first male to become Muslim and pray immediately." Ibn Abi Shayba also records that 'Abdullah ibn 'Umar (may Allah be pleased with them both, and may He grant them contentment) said, "We used to always call Zayd ibn Harith "Zayd ibn Muhammad," and this continued to be the case until Allah revealed the *ayah*, 'Call them by the names of their biological fathers.'"[18]

---

(١٥) ذكره المتقي الهندي في كنز العمال (٣٩٧/١٣).

(١٦) أخرجه مسلم (٤٥٧٨).

(17) Translator's note: In other words, he was a freed slave who, by virtue of the Prophet freeing him, became a man of Qurasyh in terms of nationality. There are many other legal ramifications that occur due to someone freeing a slave, but such rulings are beyond the scope of our topic here.

(18) Surah al-Ahzab, *ayah* 5.

HADITH ELEVEN

١١- فَضْلُ أُسَامَةَ بْنِ زَيْدٍ رَضِيَ اللهُ عَنْهُمَا: أَخْرَجَ التِّرْمِذِيُّ وَصَحَّحَهُ عَنْ أُسَامَةَ بْنِ زَيْدٍ رَضِيَ اللهُ عَنْهُمَا قَالَ: كُنْتُ جَالِسًا إِذْ جَاءَ عَلِيٌّ وَالعَبَّاسُ يَسْتَأْذِنَانِ، فَقَالَا: يَا أُسَامَةُ اسْتَأْذِنْ لَنَا عَلَى رَسُولِ اللهِ صَلَّى اللهُ عَلَيْهِ وَسَلَّمَ، فَقُلْتُ: يَا رَسُولَ اللهِ عَلِيٌّ وَالعَبَّاسُ يَسْتَأْذِنَانِ، قَالَ: «أَتَدْرِي مَا جَاءَ بِهِمَا؟» قُلْتُ: لَا، قَالَ النَّبِيُّ صَلَّى اللهُ عَلَيْهِ وَسَلَّمَ: «لَكِنِّي أَدْرِي، ائْذَنْ لَهُمَا»، فَدَخَلَا، فَقَالَا: يَا رَسُولَ اللهِ جِئْنَاكَ نَسْأَلُكَ أَيُّ أَهْلِكَ أَحَبُّ إِلَيْكَ؟ قَالَ: «فَاطِمَةُ بِنْتُ مُحَمَّدٍ»، قَالَا: مَا جِئْنَاكَ نَسْأَلُكَ عَنْ أَهْلِكَ. قَالَ: «فَأَحَبُّ النَّاسِ إِلَيَّ مَنْ أَنْعَمَ اللهُ عَلَيْهِ وَأَنْعَمْتُ عَلَيْهِ أُسَامَةُ بْنُ زَيْدٍ». قَالَا: ثُمَّ مَنْ؟ قَالَ: «ثُمَّ عَلِيُّ بْنُ أَبِي طَالِبٍ». قَالَ العَبَّاسُ: يَا رَسُولَ اللهِ جَعَلْتَ عَمَّكَ آخِرَهُمْ؟ قَالَ: «إِنَّ عَلِيًّا سَبَقَكَ بِالهِجْرَةِ» ⁽¹⁹⁾.

On the stature of Osama ibn Zayd (may Allah be pleased with them both, and may He grant them contentment), Imam at-Tirmithi narrates a rigorously authenticated hadith that is from Osama ibn Zayd himself (may Allah be pleased with them both, and may He grant them contentment). Osama says therein, "I was once sitting when all of a sudden 'Ali and 'Abbas (may Allah be pleased with them both, and may He grant them contentment) came to the Prophet's house seeking entry from me. I informed the Prophet saying, 'Oh Messenger of Allah, 'Ali and 'Abbas have come seeking permission to visit you.' 'Do you know what has brought them

---

(١٩) أخرجه الترمذي (٣٩١٥).

here?' asked the Prophet (may Allah bless him, and may He grant him peace). I responded, 'No.' The Prophet (may Allah bless him, and may He grant him peace) then said, 'Yet, I know. Well then, let them in.' As soon as they entered, they asked the Prophet (may Allah bless him, and may He grant him peace), 'Oh Emissary of Allah! We have come to ask you which member of your family is most beloved to you.' 'Fatima bint Muhammad,' the Prophet (may Allah bless him, and may He grant him peace) answered. 'We have not come to ask you about your children,' they said. 'Well, the most beloved of all people to me is one who Allah has shown His favor to and one whom I have also showered my favor upon him, and he is Osama ibn Zayd,' the Prophet responded. 'After him, then who?' they continued. 'Then 'Ali ibn Abi Talib,' said the Prophet (may Allah bless him, and may He grant him peace). Al-'Abbas then asked reluctantly, 'Oh Messenger of Allah, have you made your uncle the last of them?' "'Ali preceded you in migrating *[al-hijra]* to Madina,' the Prophet (may Allah bless him, and may He grant him peace) explained."

HADITH TWELVE

١٢- فَضْلُ حَمْزَةَ رَضِيَ اللَّهُ عَنْهُ: أَخْرَجَ الطَّبَرَانِيُّ عَنْ جَابِرٍ قَالَ: لَمَّا قُتِلَ حَمْزَةُ يَوْمَ أُحُدٍ أَقْبَلَتْ صَفِيَّةُ تَطْلُبُهُ لَا تَدْرِي مَا صَنَعَ، فَلَقِيَتْ عَلِيًّا وَالزُّبَيْرَ، فَقَالَ عَلِيٌّ لِلزُّبَيْرِ: اذْكُرْ لِأُمِّكَ، وَقَالَ الزُّبَيْرُ لِعَلِيٍّ: اذْكُرْ أَنْتَ لِعَمَّتِكَ، قَالَتْ: مَا فَعَلَ حَمْزَةُ؟ فَأَرَيَاهَا أَنَّهُمَا لَا يَدْرِيَانِ، فَجَاءَ النَّبِيُّ صَلَّى اللَّهُ عَلَيْهِ وَسَلَّمَ فَقَالَ: «إِنِّي أَخَافُ عَلَى عَقْلِهَا»، فَوَضَعَ يَدَهُ عَلَى صَدْرِهَا، وَدَعَا فَاسْتَرْجَعَتْ وَبَكَتْ، ثُمَّ جَاءَ صَلَّى اللَّهُ عَلَيْهِ وَسَلَّمَ فَقَامَ عَلَيْهِ وَهُوَ قَدْ مُثِّلَ بِهِ، فَقَالَ: «لَوْلَا جَزَعُ النِّسَاءِ لَتَرَكْتُهُ حَتَّى يُحْشَرَ مِنْ حَوَاصِلِ الطَّيْرِ وَبُطُونِ السِّبَاعِ»، ثُمَّ أَمَرَ بِالْقَتْلَى فَجُعِلَ يُصَلِّي عَلَيْهِمْ، فَيَضَعُ سَبْعَةً وَحَمْزَةُ فَيُكَبِّرُ عَلَيْهِمْ سَبْعَ تَكْبِيرَاتٍ، ثُمَّ يُرْفَعُونَ وَيُتْرَكُ حَمْزَةُ، ثُمَّ يَضَعُ سَبْعَةً فَيُكَبِّرُ عَلَيْهِمْ سَبْعَ تَكْبِيرَاتٍ، حَتَّى فَرَغَ مِنْهُمْ (٢٠).

On the virtues of Hamza (may Allah be pleased with him, and may He grant him contentment), Imam at-Tabarani records for us that Jabir ibn 'Abdillah (may Allah be pleased with him, and may He grant him contentment) said, "When Hamza was martyred during the Battle of Uhud, Safiyya (bint 'Abd al-Muttalib)[21] came forth looking for him, because she did not know what happened to him. She finally met up with 'Ali and az-Zubayr (may Allah be pleased with

---

(٢٠) أخرجه الطبراني في الكبير (٢٨٦٦).

(21) This Safiyya was Hamza's sister and the aunt of Prophet (may Allah bless him, and may He grant him peace) and 'Ali (may Allah be pleased with him, and may He grant him contentment). She was close to Hamza because, along with being children of 'Abd al-Muttalib, they also shared the same mother, Halala bint Wuhayb.

them, and may He grant them contentment) when 'Ali told az-Zubayr, 'Tell your mother what has happened.' Az-Zubayr responded, 'She is your aunt, you can inform her of what happened.' Safiyya finally asked, 'Where has Hamza gone?' 'Ali and Zubayr told her that they did not know what happened; just then, the Prophet (may Allah bless him, and may He grant him peace) arrived and said, 'Really, I fear that she may go crazy if she finds out.' The Prophet (may Allah bless him, and may He grant him peace) then placed his hand on her chest and prayed for her. She then exclaimed, 'Indeed, we are from Allah and to Him we return!' and she began to weep intensely. When the Prophet (may Allah bless him, and may He grant him peace) located Hamza's body, he found that it had been desecrated, and he said, 'If it were not for the distress that the women would experience, I would leave him here so that he could be resurrected from the innards of raptors and the stomachs of wild beasts.' He then commanded that the martyrs be brought forth so that he could perform the funeral prayer for them. Before the first funeral prayer seven bodies were brought forth along with Hamza's. After the Prophet (may Allah bless him, and may He grant him peace) said 'Allah is the Great,' *[Allah Akbar]* seven times, these seven bodies would be removed, but Hamza's body was left to the effect that each time seven new bodies were brought forth, Hamza's body was with theirs and received burial rights repeatedly in such a fashion until all the bodies had the funeral prayer performed upon them."

HADITH THIRTEEN

١٣- فَضْلُ العَبَّاسِ رَضِيَ اللهُ عَنْهُ: أَخْرَجَ الحَاكِمُ وَغَيْرُهُ عَنِ ابْنِ عُمَرَ رَضِيَ اللهُ عَنْهُمَا قَالَ: اِسْتَسْقَى عُمَرُ عَامَ الرَّمَادَةِ بِالعَبَّاسِ بْنِ عَبْدِ المُطَّلِبِ، فَقَالَ: اللَّهُمَّ هَذَا عَمُّ نَبِيِّكَ صَلَّى اللهُ عَلَيْهِ وَسَلَّمَ، نَتَوَجَّهُ إِلَيْكَ بِهِ فَاسْقِنَا، فَمَا بَرِحُوا حَتَّى سَقَاهُمُ اللهُ، فَخَطَبَ عُمَرُ النَّاسَ، فَقَالَ: أَيُّهَا النَّاسُ، إِنَّ رَسُولَ اللهِ صَلَّى اللهُ عَلَيْهِ وَسَلَّمَ كَانَ يَرَى لِلْعَبَّاسِ مَا يَرَى الوَلَدُ لِوَالِدِهِ، يُعَظِّمُهُ وَيُفَخِّمُهُ وَيَبَرُّ قَسَمَهُ، فَاقْتَدُوا أَيُّهَا النَّاسُ بِرَسُولِ اللهِ صَلَّى اللهُ عَلَيْهِ وَسَلَّمَ فِي عَمِّهِ العَبَّاسِ، وَاتَّخِذُوهُ وَسِيلَةً إِلَى اللهِ فِيمَا نَزَلَ بِكُمْ (٢٢).

On the merit of al-'Abbas (may Allah be pleased with him, and may He grant him contentment), al-Hakim and other hadith compilers record for us that 'Abdullah ibn 'Umar (may Allah be pleased with them both, and may He grant them contentment) said, "During the year of the Drought[23] *['am ar-ramada]* 'Umar once went out with the people to pray for rain *[salat al-istisqa']*, and he brought al-'Abbas ibn 'Abd al-Muttalib with them supplicating, 'Oh Allah! We have come in front of you today turning to You here with the uncle of Your Prophet (may Allah bless him, and may He grant him peace), so provide us with rain.' They did not leave their places of prayer before Allah Almighty

---

(٢٢) أخرجه الحاكم في المستدرك (٥٤٣٨).

(23) This year occurred during the caliphate of 'Umar ibn al-Khattab (may Allah be pleased with him, and may He grant him contentment). The scholars note that *ramada*, which means, "ash," was associated with this year because during this drought the wind blew so hard that the atmosphere felt like like ash.

descended rain. 'Umar (may Allah be pleased with him, and may He grant him contentment) then got up addressing the people, 'Oh people! Indeed, the Messenger of Allah held al-'Abbas in high esteem just as a son holds his father in high esteem respecting him, honoring him, being dutiful to him and fulfilling all his rights. So follow follow the example of Allah's Messenger as it concerns his uncle! Take this man as a means to gain closeness to Allah Almighty and a medium to attaining relief from all that which afflicts you!'"

HADITH FOURTEEN

١٤- فَضْلُ جَعْفَرٍ رَضِيَ اللهُ عَنْهُ: أَخْرَجَ الشَّيْخَانِ عَنِ البَرَاءِ بْنِ عَازِبٍ رَضِيَ اللهُ عَنْهُمَا أَنَّ النَّبِيَّ صَلَّى اللهُ عَلَيْهِ وَسَلَّمَ قَالَ لِجَعْفَرٍ: «أَشْبَهْتَ خَلْقِي وَخُلُقِي».^(٢٤)

Concerning the eminence of Ja'far ibn Abi Talib (may Allah be pleased with him, and may He grant him contentment), the two Shaykh's narrated that al-Bara' ibn 'Azib (may Allah be pleased with them both, and may He grant them contentment) said, "The Prophet (may Allah bless him, and may He grant him peace) informed Ja'far, 'You are the most like me both in terms of my physical features *[khalqi]* and my manners *[khuluqi]*.'"

(٢٤) أخرجه البخاري (٢٦٩٩).

HADITH FIFTEEN

١٥- فَضْلُ عَقِيلٍ رَضِيَ اللهُ عَنْهُ: أَخْرَجَ ابْنُ عَسَاكِرَ عَنْ عَبْدِ الرَّحْمَنِ بْنِ سَابِطٍ قَالَ: كَانَ النَّبِيُّ صَلَّى اللهُ عَلَيْهِ وَسَلَّمَ، يَقُولُ لِعَقِيلِ بْنِ أَبِي طَالِبٍ: إِنِّي لَأُحِبُّكَ حُبَّيْنِ حُبًّا لَكَ، وَحُبًّا لِحُبِّ أَبِي طَالِبٍ لَكَ»(٢٥).

وَأَخْرَجَ ابْنُ عَسَاكِرَ أَيْضاً عَنْ جَابِرٍ أَنَّ عَقِيلاً دَخَلَ عَلَى النَّبِيِّ صَلَّى اللهُ عَلَيْهِ وَسَلَّمَ، فَقَالَ لَهُ: «مَرْحَباً بِكَ أَبَا يَزِيدَ، كَيْفَ أَصْبَحْتَ؟», فَقَالَ: بِخَيْرٍ صَبَّحَكَ اللهُ يَا أَبَا القَاسِمِ(٢٦).

On the virtue of ʿAqil (may Allah be pleased with him, and may He grant him contentment), ibn ʿAsakir narrates that ʿAbdurrahman ibn Sabit said, "The Prophet (may Allah bless him, and may He grant him peace) used to tell ʿAqil ibn ʿAbd al-Muttalib, 'My love for you is twin-fold; I love you for who you are, but I also love you because of the love Abu Talib had for you.'" Ibn ʿAsakir also narrates that Jabir reported that ʿAqil once visited the Prophet (may Allah bless him, and may He grant him peace), and he said to him, "Welcome! Oh Abu Yazid, how is your morning so far?" "I am well! May Allah fill your morning with blessing, oh Abu 'l-Qasim!"

---

(٢٥) أخرجه ابن عساكر في تاريخ دمشق (٤١/١٨).

(٢٦) أخرجه ابن عساكر في تاريخ دمشق (٤١/١٧).

HADITH SIXTEEN

١٦- فَضْلُ عَبْدِ اللهِ بْنِ عَبَّاسٍ رَضِيَ اللهُ عَنْهُمَا: أَخْرَجَ ابْنُ أَبِي شَيْبَةَ عَنِ ابْنِ عَبَّاسٍ قَالَ: كُنْتُ فِي بَيْتِ مَيْمُونَةَ -يَعْنِي- خَالَتَهُ- زَوْجِ النَّبِيِّ صَلَّى اللهُ عَلَيْهِ وَسَلَّمَ فَوَضَعْتُ لِرَسُولِ اللهِ صَلَّى اللهُ عَلَيْهِ وَسَلَّمَ طَهُورَهُ، فَقَالَ: «مَنْ وَضَعَ لِي هَذَا؟» فَقَالَتْ مَيْمُونَةُ: عَبْدُ اللهِ، فَقَالَ: «اللَّهُمَّ فَقِّهْهُ فِي الدِّينِ وَعَلِّمْهُ التَّأْوِيلَ»(٢٧).

وَأَخْرَجَ ابْنُ أَبِي شَيْبَةَ أَيْضاً عَنْهُ أَنَّهُ قَالَ: دَعَا لِي رَسُولُ اللهِ صَلَّى اللهُ عَلَيْهِ وَسَلَّمَ أَنْ يَزِيدَنِي اللهُ عِلْماً وَفَهْماً، وَكَانَ عُمَرُ يَسْتَشِيرُهُ فِي الْأَمْرِ إِذَا أَهَمَّهُ(٢٨).

On the greatness of 'Abdullah ibn 'Abbas (may Allah be pleased with them both, and may He grant them contentment), ibn Abi Shayba reports for us that ibn 'Abbas said, "I was once in the apartment of Maymuna (who was ibn 'Abbas' aunt) the wife of the Prophet (may Allah bless him, and may He grant him peace), and readied the Prophet's water for his ablution. The Prophet (may Allah bless him, and may He grant him peace) asked, 'Who put this here for me?' Maymuna responded, ''Abdullah.' The Prophet (may Allah bless him, and may He grant him peace) then supplicated, 'Oh Allah! Give him understanding of this religion, and teach him the art of interpretation.'" Ibn Abi Shayba also recorded from ibn 'Abbas said, "Allah's Emissary Allah (may

---

(٢٧) أخرجه ابن أبي شيبة في مصنفه (٥٢٠/٧).

(٢٨) أخرجه ابن أبي شيبة في مصنفه (١٣٥٤٢)، وأحمد في فضائل الصحابة (١٦٥٥).

Allah bless him, and may He grant him peace) prayed to Allah on my behalf that He endow me with knowledge and deep understanding." Indeed, as it became the case later on, 'Umar ibn al-Khattab (may Allah be pleased with him, and may He grant him contentment) would seek the council of 'ibn 'Abbas concerning any grave matter.

HADITH SEVENTEEN

١٧- فَضْلُ طَلْحَةَ رَضِيَ اللهُ عَنْهُ: أَخْرَجَ التِّرْمِذِيُّ عَنِ الزُّبَيْرِ بْنِ العَوَّامِ رَضِيَ اللهُ عَنْهُ قَالَ: كَانَ عَلَى النَّبِيِّ صَلَّى اللهُ عَلَيْهِ وَسَلَّمَ يَوْمَ أُحُدٍ دِرْعَانِ، فَنَهَضَ إِلَى الصَّخْرَةِ فَلَمْ يَسْتَطِعْ، فَقَعَدَ طَلْحَةُ تَحْتَهُ حَتَّى اسْتَوَى عَلَى الصَّخْرَةِ، فَسَمِعْتُ رَسُولَ اللهِ صَلَّى اللهُ عَلَيْهِ وَسَلَّمَ يَقُولُ: «أَوْجَبَ طَلْحَةُ» أَيْ: الجَنَّةَ, كَمَا فِي رِوَايَةٍ(٢٩).

وَأَخْرَجَ البُخَارِيُّ عَنْ قَيْسِ بْنِ حَازِمٍ قَالَ: رَأَيْتُ يَدَ طَلْحَةَ شَلَّاءَ وَقَى بِهَا النَّبِيَّ صَلَّى اللهُ عَلَيْهِ وَسَلَّمَ يَوْمَ أُحُدٍ(٣٠).

Concerning the excellence of Talha (may Allah be pleased with him, and may He grant him contentment), Imam at-Tirmithi reported that az-Zubayr ibn al-'Awwam (may Allah be pleased with him, and may He grant him contentment) narrated, "During the Battle of Uhud, the Prophet (may Allah bless him, and may He grant him peace) wore two coats of mail. At a point in the battle he became exhausted and attempted to climb a rock, but he was unable to keep himself balanced, so Talha came forth and got under the Prophet helping him gain his balance and mount the rock. It was at this moment when I heard the Prophet (may Allah bless him, and may He grant him peace) say, 'Talha has now made it necessary.'" In another narration there is the addition

---

(٢٩) أخرجه الترمذي (١٦٩٢).

(٣٠) أخرجه البخاري (٤٠٦٣).

of "(made) his entry into paradise necessary." Imam al-Bukhari also verifies a narration in which Qays ibn Hazim informs us, "I saw Talha during the Battle of Uhud with his hand paralyzed but still using it to protect the Prophet (may Allah bless him, and may He grant him peace)."

HADITH EIGHTEEN

١٨- فَضْلُ الزُّبَيْرِ رَضِيَ اللهُ عَنْهُ: أَخْرَجَ الشَّيْخَانِ عَنْ جَابِرٍ رَضِيَ اللهُ عَنْهُ قَالَ: قَالَ النَّبِيُّ صَلَّى اللهُ عَلَيْهِ وَسَلَّمَ: «مَنْ يَأْتِينِي بِخَبَرِ القَوْمِ يَوْمَ الأَحْزَابِ؟» قَالَ الزُّبَيْرُ: أَنَا، فَقَالَ النَّبِيُّ صَلَّى اللهُ عَلَيْهِ وَسَلَّمَ: «إِنَّ لِكُلِّ نَبِيٍّ حَوَارِيًّا، وَحَوَارِيَّ الزُّبَيْرُ» (٣١). وَمَعْنَى الحَوَارِيِّ: النَّاصِرُ.

On the virtue of az-Zubayr (may Allah be pleased with him, and may He grant him contentment), the two Shaykhs report for us that Jabir narrated that the Prophet (may Allah bless him, and may He grant him peace) once asked, "Who will bring the news of those people?" After which, az-Zubayr immediately stood up and said, "I will." "Indeed, every prophet has an apostle [hawwari] who helps him to victory and my apostle is az-Zubayr," the Prophet (may Allah bless him, and may He grant him peace) affirmed. Among the meanings of "hawwari" in the Arabic language is "supporter."

---

(٣١) أخرجه البخاري (٢٨٤٦).

HADITH NINETEEN

١٩- فَضْلُ سَعْدِ بْنِ أَبِي وَقَّاصٍ رَضِيَ اللهُ عَنْهُ: أَخْرَجَ الشَّيْخَانِ عَنْ عَلِيٍّ رَضِيَ اللهُ عَنْهُ قَالَ: مَا سَمِعْتُ النَّبِيَّ صَلَّى اللهُ عَلَيْهِ وَسَلَّمَ جَمَعَ أَبَوَيْهِ لِأَحَدٍ إِلَّا لِسَعْدِ بْنِ مَالِكٍ, فَإِنِّي سَمِعْتُهُ يَقُولُ يَوْمَ أُحُدٍ: «ارْمِ فِدَاكَ أَبِي وَأُمِّي» (٣٢).

The two Shaykh's quote 'Ali (may Allah ennoble his countenance) concerning the distinction of Sa'd ibn Abi Waqqas (may Allah be pleased with him, and may He grant him contentment). 'Ali informs us, "I never heard the Prophet (may Allah bless him, and may He grant him peace) say that he would give both his parents in ransom for anyone except Sa'd ibn Abi Waqqas (may Allah be pleased with him, and may He grant him contentment). Indeed, I heard the Prophet exclaim during the Battle of Uhud, 'Fight on! Let my father and my mother be your ransom.'"

---

(٣٢) أخرجه البخاري (٢٧٤٩) ومسلم (٢٤١١).

HADITH TWENTY

٢٠- فَضْلُ أَبِي عُبَيْدَةَ رَضِيَ اللهُ عَنْهُ: أَخْرَجَ الشَّيْخَانِ عَنْ أَنَسٍ قَالَ: قَالَ رَسُوْلُ اللهِ صَلَّى اللهُ عَلَيْهِ وَسَلَّمَ: «لِكُلِّ أُمَّةٍ أَمِيْنٌ، وَأَمِيْنُ هَذِهِ الأُمَّةِ أَبُوْ عُبَيْدَةَ بْنُ الجَرَّاحِ». (٣٣)

On the excellence of Abu 'Ubayda ibn al-Jarrah (may Allah be pleased with him, and may He grant him contentment), the two Shaykhs record for us that Anas narrated, "The Messenger of Allah (may Allah bless him, and may He grant him peace) said, 'Every nation has its trustee *[amin]*, and the trustee of this nation is Abu 'Ubayda ibn al-Jarrah.'"

(٣٣) أخرجه البخاري (٧٢٥٥).

HADITH TWENTY-ONE

٢١- فَضْلُ عَبْدِ الرَّحْمَنِ بْنِ عَوْفٍ رَضِيَ اللهُ عَنْهُ: أَخْرَجَ الإِمَامُ أَحْمَدُ عَنْ أُمِّ سَلَمَةَ رَضِيَ اللهُ عَنْهَا قَالَتْ: سَمِعْتُ رَسُولَ اللهِ صَلَّى اللهُ عَلَيْهِ وَسَلَّمَ يَقُولُ لِأَزْوَاجِهِ: «إِنَّ الَّذِي يَحْنُو عَلَيْكُنَّ بَعْدِي هُوَ الصَّادِقُ البَارُّ، اللَّهُمَّ اسْقِ عَبْدَ الرَّحْمَنِ بْنَ عَوْفٍ مِنْ سَلْسَبِيلِ الجَنَّةِ» (٣٤).

وَرَوَى التِّرْمِذِيُّ أَنَّ عَائِشَةَ رَضِيَ اللهُ عَنْهَا قَالَتْ لِابْنِهِ أَبِي سَلَمَةَ: «سَقَى اللهُ أَبَاكَ مِنْ سَلْسَبِيلِ الجَنَّةِ» (٣٥). وَكَانَ ابْنُ عَوْفٍ قَدْ تَصَدَّقَ عَلَى أُمَّهَاتِ المُؤْمِنِينَ بِحَدِيقَةٍ بِيعَتْ بِأَرْبَعِينَ أَلْفاً.

Imam Ahmad records the following hadith from Umm Salama (may Allah be pleased with her, and may He grant her contentment), who extols the merits of 'Abdurrahman ibn 'Awf (may Allah be pleased with him, and may He grant him contentment). She says, "I once heard the Messenger of Allah (may Allah bless him, and may He grant him peace) telling his wives, 'He who will look after you after me is a man of honor, honesty and integrity. Oh Allah! Give 'Abdurrahman ibn 'Awf a drink from the sweet waters of paradise.'" Additionally, Imam at-Tirmithi recorded that 'Aisha (may Allah be pleased with her, and may He grant her contentment) said to ('Abdurrahman ibn 'Awfs daughter), "Allah endowed your father with a drink from

---

(٣٤) أخرجه أحمد (٢٥٧٧٤).

(٣٥) أخرجه الترمذي (٣٧٤٩).

the sweet waters of paradise." It is noted in the history books that 'Abdurrahman ibn 'Awf sold a garden for 40,000 gold pieces, and it was from this that he paid for the upkeep of the the mothers of the believers, i.e. the Prophet's wives.

HADITH TWENTY-TWO

٢٢- فَضْلُ سَعِيدِ بْنِ زَيْدٍ رَضِيَ اللهُ عَنْهُ: أَخْرَجَ التِّرْمِذِيُّ وَصَحَّحَهُ عَنْ سَعِيدِ بْنِ زَيْدٍ قَالَ: أَشْهَدُ عَلَى التِّسْعَةِ أَنَّهُمْ فِي الجَنَّةِ، وَلَوْ شَهِدْتُ عَلَى العَاشِرِ لَمْ آثَمْ. قِيلَ لَهُ: وَكَيْفَ ذَاكَ ؟ قَالَ: كُنَّا مَعَ رَسُولِ اللهِ صَلَّى اللهُ عَلَيْهِ وَسَلَّمَ بِحِرَاءَ فَتَحَرَّكَ فَضَرَبَهُ بِرِجْلِهِ، ثُمَّ قَالَ: «اُثْبُتْ حِرَاءُ، فَإِنَّهُ لَيْسَ عَلَيْكَ إِلَّا نَبِيٌّ أَوْ صِدِّيقٌ أَوْ شَهِيدٌ». قِيلَ: وَمَنْ هُمْ ؟ فَعَدَّ التِّسْعَةَ. قِيلَ: فَمَنِ العَاشِرُ ؟ قَالَ: أَنَا(٣٦).

وَفِي رِوَايَةِ ابْنِ عَسَاكِرَ: وَلَوْ شِئْتُ أَنْ أُسَمِّيَ العَاشِرَ لَسَمَّيْتُهُ, قِيلَ: عَزَمْتُ عَلَيْكَ لَتُسَمِّيَنَّهُ, قَالَ: أَنَا(٣٧).

Concerning the virtues of Saʿid ibn Zayd (may Allah be pleased with him, and may He grant him contentment), Imam at-Tirmithi narrates a hadith that he also grades as being authentic. He quotes Saʿid ibn Zayd as saying, "I can bear witness to nine people being in paradise, and if I were to testify to a tenth person being among them I would not be blameworthy." He was asked, "Elaborate for us, how is that so?" He responded, "We were with the Messenger of Allah (may Allah bless him, and may He grant him peace) above the cave of Hiraʾ when it began to shake, and the Prophet stomped on it with his foot saying, 'Be steady, oh Hiraʾ! For indeed, there is a prophet, a trust-worthy [siddiq] one and

---

(٣٦) أخرجه الترمذي (٤٠٦٤).

(٣٧) أخرجه ابن عساكر في تاريخ دمشق (١٨/٣٩٠).

martyr above you!'" He was asked, "Who are the nine?" After he named them, he was asked, "Then who is the tenth one?" "I am," he responded. In another version of the same event recorded by ibn 'Asakir, Sa'id ibn Zayd says, "If I wanted to, I would name the tenth person for you." A question then said to him, "I am determined that you will name who he is!" Finally, Sa'id (may Allah be pleased with him, and may He grant him contentment) informed them all, "I am."

HADITH TWENTY-THREE

٢٣- فَضْلُ عَبْدِ اللهِ بْنِ مَسْعُودٍ رَضِيَ اللهُ عَنْهُ: أَخْرَجَ البُخَارِيُّ عَنْ حُذَيْفَةَ قَالَ: إنَّ أَشْبَهَ النَّاسِ دَلًّا وَسَمْتًا وَهَدْيًا بِرَسُولِ اللهِ صَلَّى اللهُ عَلَيْهِ وَسَلَّمَ لَابْنُ أُمِّ عَبْدٍ، مِنْ حِينِ يَخْرُجُ مِنْ بَيْتِهِ إلَى أَنْ يَرْجِعَ إِلَيْهِ، لاَ نَدْرِي مَا يَصْنَعُ فِي أَهْلِهِ إِذَا خَلاَ (٣٨).

وَأَخْرَجَ الشَّيْخَانِ عَنْ عَبْدِ اللهِ بْنِ عَمْرٍو أَنَّ رَسُولَ اللهِ صَلَّى اللهُ عَلَيْهِ وَسَلَّمَ قَالَ: «اسْتَقْرِئُوا القُرْآنَ مِنْ أَرْبَعَةٍ: مِنْ عَبْدِ اللهِ بْنِ مَسْعُودٍ، وَسَالِمٍ مَوْلَى أَبِي حُذَيْفَةَ، وَأُبَيِّ بْنِ كَعْبٍ، وَمُعَاذِ بْنِ جَبَلٍ» (٣٩).

The excellence of 'Abdullah ibn Mas'ud is illustrated in a narration recorded by Imam al-Bukhari, who quotes Huthayfa (may Allah be pleased with him, and may He grant him contentment) as having said, "Verily, out of all people, ibn Mas'ud is the most similar to the Prophet (may Allah bless him, and may He grant him peace) in terms of his bearing, dignified conduct and exemplification of the prophetic guidance; I can vouch for him in those regards based on all that I have seen while he leaves his house until he returns home – given that we have no knowledge of the inner affairs of his household." The two Shaykhs both recorded and verified another narration in which 'Abdullah ibn 'Amr said, "Seek out the Qur'an from four people: 'Abdullah ibn Mas'ud, Salim (the client of Abi Huthayfa), Ubayy ibn Ka'b and Mu'ath ibn Jabal."

---

(٣٨) أخرجه البخاري (٦٠٩٧).

(٣٩) أخرجه البخاري (٣٥٠١) ومسلم (٢٤٦٤).

HADITH TWENTY-FOUR

٢٤- فَضْلُ عَبْدِ اللهِ بْنِ جَحْشٍ رَضِيَ اللهُ عَنْهُ: أَخْرَجَ ابْنُ أَبِي شَيْبَةَ عَنْ سَعْدِ بْنِ أَبِي وَقَّاصٍ رَضِيَ اللهُ عَنْهُ أَنَّ رَسُوْلَ اللهِ صَلَّى اللهُ عَلَيْهِ وَسَلَّمَ أَمَّرَ عَبْدَ اللهِ بْنَ جَحْشٍ, وَكَانَ أَوَّلَ أَمِيْرٍ أُمِّرَ فِي الْإِسْلَامِ(٤٠).

The merit of 'Abdullah ibn Jahsh is captured in a narration recorded and verified by ibn Abi Shayba who quoted Sa'id ibn Abi Waqqas (may Allah be pleased with him, and may He grant him contentment) as saying, "Verily, the Messenger of Allah (may Allah bless him, and may He grant him peace) made 'Abdullah ibn Jahsh a general of his troops, and like this, he was the first person to ever be put in a position of leadership by the Prophet (may Allah bless him, and may He grant him peace)."

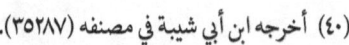

(٤٠) أخرجه ابن أبي شيبة في مصنفه (٣٥٢٨٧).

HADITH TWENTY-FIVE

٢٥- فَضْلُ مُصْعَبٍ رَضِيَ اللهُ عَنْهُ: أَخْرَجَ الْحَاكِمُ وَغَيْرُهُ عَنْ عُمَرَ رَضِيَ اللهُ عَنْهُ قَالَ: نَظَرَ رَسُولُ اللهِ صَلَّى اللهُ عَلَيْهِ وَسَلَّمَ إِلَى مُصْعَبِ بْنِ عُمَيْرٍ مُقْبِلًا، عَلَيْهِ إِهَابُ كَبْشٍ قَدْ تَنَطَّقَ بِهِ، فَقَالَ النَّبِيُّ صَلَّى اللهُ عَلَيْهِ وَسَلَّمَ: «اُنْظُرُوا إِلَى هَذَا الَّذِي نَوَّرَ اللهُ قَلْبَهُ، لَقَدْ رَأَيْتُهُ بَيْنَ أَبَوَيْنِ يُغَذِّوَانَهُ بِأَطْيَبِ الطَّعَامِ وَالشَّرَابِ، وَلَقَدْ رَأَيْتُ عَلَيْهِ حُلَّةً اشْتُرِيَتْ بِمِأَتَيْ دِرْهَمٍ فَدَعَاهُ حُبُّ اللهِ وَحُبُّ رَسُولِهِ إِلَى مَا تَرَوْنَ».⁽⁴¹⁾

Al-Hakim and others narrate a hadith concerning the virtue of Musʻab ibn ʻUmayr. They quote ʻUmar ibn al-Khattab (may Allah be pleased with him, and may He grant him contentment) as having said, "The Messenger of Allah (may Allah bless him, and may He grant him peace) once looked at Musʻab ibn ʻUmayr from a distance as Musʻab approached him lugging a sheep's skin around his shoulders. As he drew closer, the Prophet (may Allah bless him, and may He grant him peace) said to his companions around him, 'Look at this fine young man; Allah has put the light of faith in his heart. Not too long ago, I witnessed his parents provide for him and pamper him with the best of food and expensive drink – along with clothing him in the finest garments. I used to see him wearing a necklace that he later sold for 200 gold pieces. Now, his love for Allah and His Emissary has spurred him to abandon that life of luxury for the state that you now see him in."⁴²

---

(٤١) أخرجه البيهقي في شعب الإيمان (٥٧٠٧), وأبو نعيم في الحلية (٣٣٥).

(42) Translator's note: The Prophet (may Allah bless him, and may He grant

HADITH TWENTY-SIX

٢٦- فَضْلُ خَالِدِ بْنِ الوَلِيدِ رَضِيَ اللهُ عَنْهُ: أَخْرَجَ الإِمَامُ أَحْمَدُ وَغَيْرُهُ عَنْ أَبِي بَكْرٍ الصِّدِّيقِ رَضِيَ اللهُ عَنْهُ قَالَ: سَمِعْتُ رَسُولَ اللهِ صَلَّى اللَّهُ عَلَيْهِ وَسَلَّمَ يَقُولُ وَذَكَرَ خَالِدَ بْنَ الوَلِيدِ قَالَ: «نِعْمَ عَبْدُ اللَّهِ وَأَخُو العَشِيرَةِ سَيْفٌ مِنْ سُيُوفِ اللَّهِ، سَلَّهُ اللهُ عَلَى الكُفَّارِ وَالْمُنَافِقِينَ» (٤٣).

On the supremacy of Khalid ibn al-Walid (may Allah be pleased with him, and may He grant him contentment), Imam Ahmad recorded that Abi Bakr as-Siddiq (may Allah be pleased with him, and may He grant him contentment) said, "I heard the Messenger of Allah (may Allah bless him, and may He grant him peace) describing Khalid ibn al-Walid, "This fine slave of Allah and Arab chieftan is a sword from among the swords that Allah has unsheathed upon the disbelievers and the hypocrites."

---

him peace) here makes reference to Mus'ab's parents opposing his conversion to Islam and threatening to leave him poor. So Mus'ab (may Allah be pleased with him, and may He grant him contentment) gave up his former life luxury to practice his faith without opposition.

(٤٣) أخرجه أحمد (٢٥٧٧٤).

HADITH TWENTY-SEVEN

٢٧- فَضْلُ أَبِي ذَرٍّ رَضِيَ اللهُ عَنْهُ: أَخْرَجَ أَبُو نُعَيْمٍ عَنْ أَبِي هُرَيْرَةَ رَضِيَ اللهُ عَنْهُ قَالَ: قَالَ رَسُولُ اللهِ صَلَّى اللهُ عَلَيْهِ وَسَلَّمَ: «مَا أَظَلَّتِ الْخَضْرَاءُ وَلَا أَقَلَّتِ الْغَبْرَاءُ مِنْ ذِي لَهْجَةٍ أَصْدَقَ مِنْ أَبِي ذَرٍّ، مَنْ سَرَّهُ أَنْ يَنْظُرَ إِلَى تَوَاضُعِ عِيسَى ابْنِ مَرْيَمَ فَلْيَنْظُرْ إِلَى أَبِي ذَرٍّ» وَفِي لَفْظٍ: «أَشْبَهُ النَّاسِ بِعِيسَى نُسُكاً وَزُهْداً وَبِرّاً». وَأَخْرَجَ نَحْوَهُ التِّرْمِذِيُّ عَنْ أَبِي ذَرٍّ وَعَنْ عَبْدِ اللهِ بْنِ عُمَرَ (٤٤).

Abu Nu'aym al-Asfahani recording the following hadith concerning the virtue of Abu Tharr al-Ghifari (may Allah be pleased with him, and may He grant him contentment). He quotes Abu Hurayra (may Allah be pleased with him, and may He grant him contentment) as saying, "The Messenger of Allah (may Allah bless him, and may He grant him peace) told us, "There is no man of eloquence[45] more profoundly genuine than Abu Tharr. Further, those of you who wishto capture the simplicity and humility *[tawadu']* of 'Isa ibn Maryam, then he should look upon Abu Tharr (may Allah be pleased with him, and may He grant him contentment)."

---

(٤٤) أخرجه الترمذي (٤١٧٢), وأبو نعيم في معرفة الصحابة (٥/١١).

(45) The reference here is to the fact that those of profound eloquence usually use this skill to benefit themselves by lying, telling half-truths and manipulating the hearts of people; but not so was the case with Abu Tharr (may Allah be pleased with him, and may He grant him contentment).

HADITH TWENTY-EIGHT

٢٨- فَضْلُ المِقْدَادِ بْنِ الأَسْوَدِ رَضِيَ اللهُ عَنْهُ: أَخْرَجَ التِّرْمِذِيُّ عَنْ بُرَيْدَةَ رَضِيَ اللهُ عَنْهُ قَالَ: قَالَ رَسُوْلُ اللهِ صَلَّى اللهُ عَلَيْهِ وَسَلَّمَ: «إِنَّ اللهَ أَمَرَنِي بِحُبِّ أَرْبَعَةٍ وَأَخْبَرَنِي أَنَّهُ يُحِبُّهُمْ». قِيْلَ: يَا رَسُوْلَ اللهِ سَمِّهِمْ لَنَا, قَالَ: «عَلِيٌّ مِنْهُمْ -يَقُوْلُ ذَلِكَ ثَلَاثاً- وَأَبُوْ ذَرٍّ وَالمِقْدَادُ وَسَلْمَانُ» (٤٦).

Imam at-Tirmithi records for us the merit of the companion al-Miqdad ibn al-Aswad (may Allah be pleased with him, and may He grant him contentment) by quoting Burayda ibn al-Khasib, who said, "The Messenger of Allah (may Allah be pleased with him, and may He grant him contentment) said, 'Indeed, it is the case that Allah has commanded me to love four people, and He has also informed me that He loves these people Himself.' The companions then asked the Prophet (may Allah bless him, and may He grant him peace), 'Name them for us, oh Messenger of Allah!' ''Ali is among them (the Prophet was to repeat this three times before mentioning the last three), and Abu Tharr, Miqdad and Salman are, too.'"

---

(٤٦) أخرجه الترمذي (٣٧١٨).

HADITH TWENTY-NINE

٢٩- فَضْلُ عَمَّارِ بْنِ يَاسِرٍ رَضِيَ اللهُ عَنْهُمَا: أَخْرَجَ الإِمَامُ أَحْمَدُ وَالتِّرْمِذِيُّ وَقَالَ: حَسَنٌ صَحِيحٌ، عَنْ عَلِيٍّ رَضِيَ اللهُ عَنْهُ قَالَ: كُنَّا جُلُوساً عِنْدَ النَّبِيِّ صَلَّى اللهُ عَلَيْهِ وَسَلَّمَ فَجَاءَ عَمَّارٌ يَسْتَأْذِنُ فَعَرَفَ صَوْتَهُ، فَقَالَ: «ائْذَنُوا لَهُ», فَلَمَّا دَخَلَ قَالَ: «مَرْحَباً بِالطَّيِّبِ المُطَيَّبِ» (٤٧).

وَأَخْرَجَ الإِمَامُ أَحْمَدُ وَغَيْرُهُ عَنْ عُثْمَانَ بْنِ عَفَّانَ رَضِيَ اللهُ عَنْهُمَا أَنَّهُ قَالَ: أَلَا أُحَدِّثُكُمْ عَنْهُ -يَعْنِي: عَمَّاراً- أَقْبَلْتُ مَعَ رَسُولِ اللهِ صَلَّى اللهُ عَلَيْهِ وَسَلَّمَ آخِذاً بِيَدِي يَمْشِي فِي البَطْحَاءِ حَتَّى أَتَى عَلَى أَبِيهِ وَأُمِّهِ وَعَلَيْهِ وَهُمْ يُعَذَّبُونَ, فَقَالَ عَمَّارٌ: يَا رَسُولَ اللهِ, الدَّهْرُ هَكَذَا, فَقَالَ لَهُ النَّبِيُّ صَلَّى اللهُ عَلَيْهِ وَسَلَّمَ: «اصْبِرْ», ثُمَّ قَالَ: «اللَّهُمَّ اغْفِرْ لِآلِ يَاسِرٍ وَقَدْ فَعَلْتَ» (٤٨).

وَفِي رِوَايَةٍ فَقَالَ: «صَبْراً آلَ يَاسِرٍ فَإِنَّ مَصِيرَكُمْ إِلَى الجَنَّةِ», وَذَلِكَ فِي مَكَّةَ فِي أَوَّلِ الإِسْلَامِ (٤٩).

Imam Ahmad and at-Tirmithi both document a hadith concerning the excellence of 'Ammar bin Yasir (may Allah be pleased with him, and may He grant him contentment). Consequently, at-Tirmithi was to verify this hadith as being authentic – although not rigorously authentic - in its chain

---

(٤٧) أخرجه الترمذي (٤١٦٧) وأحمد (١٠٧٣).

(٤٨) أخرجه البخاري (٣٠٦٥) وأحمد (٤٢٩).

(٤٩) أخرجه أبو نعيم في معرفة الصحابة (٣٤٤/١٩).

of narrators.[50] They quote 'Ali (may Allah be pleased with him, and may He grant him contentment) as saying, "We were once sitting in the presence of the Prophet (may Allah bless him, and may He grant him peace) when 'Ammar came seeking entrance, and we recognized his voice. The Prophet (may Allah bless him, and may He grant him peace) said, 'Allow him to enter.' When he entered, the Prophet (may Allah bless him, and may He grant him peace) said, 'Greetings! Oh blessed one! You are splendid, and you refresh others with your presence!'" Additionally, by way of another narration, Imam Ahmad and others quote 'Uthman ibn 'Affan, as having, "Shall I inform you of who this man was (intending 'Ammar)? The Messenger of Allah (may Allah bless him, and may He grant him peace) once took me by the hand and led me out to the desert flats. We walked until we saw 'Ammar, his father and his mother being tortured. As 'Ammar saw the Prophet, he said, 'Oh Messenger of Allah! Must it be so?' The Prophet (may Allah bless him, and may He grant him peace) told him, 'Be patient.' He (may Allah bless him, and may He grant him peace) then supplicated, 'Oh Allah! Forgive the family of Yasir; indeed, You have already done so.'" In another narration, the Prophet (may

---

(50) Imam at-Tirmithi verified this hadith as being of a level of authenticity, i.e. *[hassan sahih]*, just below that of rigorous authenticity *[sahih]*. This is due to this hadith's chain of narrators not meeting one or more condition out of the five conditions which he set for a hadith to be rigorously authentic. Although the scholars disagree over the term *hasan sahih*, many of them have said that the narrators of such a hadith are mixed with those of *sahih* distinction and those whose hadith would be regarded as *hasan* (acceptable). Allah knows best, but, as can be easily deduced, this narration is of enough authenticity to be taken, narrated and benefited from. And, of course, Allah is more knowledgeable of all such affairs.

Allah bless him, and may He grant him peace) was reported to have said, "Have patience, dear family of Yasir; indeed, your path to paradise has already been laid down." These events took place in Mecca during the early years of Islam.

HADITH THIRTY

٣٠- فَضْلُ بِلَالٍ رَضِيَ اللهُ عَنْهُ: أَخْرَجَ ابْنُ أَبِي شَيْبَةَ عَنْ بُرَيْدَةَ بْنِ الْخَصِيبِ الْأَسْلَمِيِّ أَنَّ رَسُولَ اللهِ صَلَّى اللهُ عَلَيْهِ وَسَلَّمَ قَالَ: «سَمِعْتُ خَشْخَشَةً أَمَامِي» فَقُلْتُ: مَنْ هَذَا ؟ قَالُوا: بِلَالٌ, قُلْتُ: «بِمَ سَبَقْتَنِي إِلَى الْجَنَّةِ؟» قَالَ: يَا رَسُولَ اللهِ مَا أَحْدَثْتُ إِلَّا تَوَضَّأْتُ, وَلَا تَوَضَّأْتُ إِلَّا رَأَيْتُ أَنَّ لِلهِ عَلَيَّ رَكْعَتَيْنِ أُصَلِّيهِمَا, قَالَ صَلَّى اللهُ عَلَيْهِ وَسَلَّمَ: «بِهَا»(٥١).

وَرَوَى الْبُخَارِيُّ عَنْ جَابِرٍ رَضِيَ اللهُ عَنْهُ قَالَ: كَانَ عُمَرُ يَقُولُ: أَبُو بَكْرٍ سَيِّدُنَا وَأَعْتَقَ سَيِّدَنَا يَعْنِي: بِلَالًا (٥٢).

Concerning the virtue of Bilal (may Allah be pleased with him, and may He grant him contentment), ibn Abi Shayba recorded that Burayda ibn al-Khasib al-Aslami said, "The Emissary of Allah (may Allah bless him, and may He grant him peace) informed us, 'I once heard the footsteps of someone in front of me, and I asked, "Who is there?" Some (beings) responded, "It is Bilal." I then later asked Bilal, "How could you have gotten into paradise before me?" He responded, "Oh Messenger of Allah! I do not break my ablution without then doing ablution again, and when I make ablutions I see it as Allah's right upon me that I pray two units of prayer."'" The Prophet (may Allah bless him, and may He grant him peace) would eventually say

---

(٥١) أخرجه ابن أبي شيبة في مصنفه (٥٣٧/٧).

(٥٢) أخرجه البخاري (٣٥٧٧).

concerning Bilal's habit, "What blessed worship!"⁵³ Imam al-Bukhari also narrates for us that 'Umar used to comment on Bilal (may Allah be pleased with both of them, and may He grant them contentment), "Our master Abu Bakr freed our master!" intending the latter to be Bilal.

---

(53) Translator's note: This last sentence from the Prophet (may Allah bless him, and may He grant him peace) is extremely concise, but abounding with meanings. So this last sentence can also be translated as, "By this gained paradise!" or "Stick to it!" which can be both be understood as the Prophet (may Allah bless him, and may He grant him peace) encouraging the believers to emulate the actions of Bilal (may Allah be pleased with him, and may He grant him contentment).

HADITH THIRTY-ONE

٣١- فَضْلُ سَعْدِ بْنِ مُعَاذٍ رَضِيَ اللّٰهُ عَنْهُ: أَخْرَجَ الْبُخَارِيُّ وَمُسْلِمٌ عَنْ جَابِرٍ رَضِيَ اللّٰهُ عَنْهُ قَالَ: سَمِعْتُ النَّبِيَّ صَلَّى اللّٰهُ عَلَيْهِ وَسَلَّمَ يَقُولُ: «اِهْتَزَّ عَرْشُ الرَّحْمٰنِ لِمَوْتِ سَعْدِ بْنِ مُعَاذٍ». وَفِي رِوَايَةٍ: «اِهْتَزَّ عَرْشُ الرَّحْمٰنِ لِسَعْدِ بْنِ مُعَاذٍ». (٥٤)

Concerning the merit of Sa'd ibn Mu'ath (may Allah be pleased with him, and may He grant him contentment), al-Bukhari and Muslim quote Jabir (may Allah be pleased with him, and may He grant him contentment) as saying, "I heard the Prophet (may Allah bless him, and may He grant him peace) say, 'The Throne of Merciful shook upon the death of Sa'd ibn Mu'ath.'" In another narration there is a variation in wording, "The Throne of Merciful has shaken because of Sa'd ibn Mu'ath."

---

(٥٤) أخرجه البخاري (٣٨٠٣) ومسلم (٢٤٦٩).

HADITH THIRTY-TWO

٣٢- فَضْلُ سَعْدِ بْنِ عُبَادَةَ رَضِيَ اللهُ عَنْهُ: أَخْرَجَ ابْنُ عَسَاكِرَ عَنْ سَعْدِ بْنِ عُبَادَةَ رَضِيَ اللهُ عَنْهُ أَنَّهُ أَتَى النَّبِيَّ صَلَّى اللهُ عَلَيْهِ وَسَلَّمَ بِصَحْفَةٍ أَوْ جَفْنَةٍ مَمْلُوءَةٍ مُخًّا, فَقَالَ: «يَا أَبَا ثَابِتٍ مَا هَذَا؟» قَالَ: وَالَّذِي بَعَثَكَ بِالحَقِّ لَقَدْ نَحَرْتُ أَرْبَعِينَ ذَاتَ كَبِدٍ فَأَحْبَبْتُ أَنْ أُشْبِعَكَ مِنَ المُخِّ, فَأَكَلَ النَّبِيُّ صَلَّى اللهُ عَلَيْهِ وَسَلَّمَ وَدَعَا لَهُ بِخَيْرٍ (٥٥).

Concerning the stature of Saʻd ibn ʻUbada (may Allah be pleased with him, and may He grant him contentment), ibn ʻAsakir quotes Saʻd ibn Ubada himself as saying that he once approached the Prophet (may Allah bless him, and may He grant him peace) with a large platter of brain and marrow. Upon his approach, the Prophet (may Allah bless him, and may He grant him peace) said, "Oh Abu Thabit, what is this?" He responded, "I swear by He who sent you in truth, I have slaughtered 40 sheep, and I desired to share with you the brain and the marrow." So the Prophet (may Allah bless him, and may He grant him peace) ate and prayed for him.

---

(٥٥) ذَكَرَهُ المُتَّقِي الهِنْدِي فِي كَنْزِ العُمَّالِ (٣٧٩/١٣).

HADITH THIRTY-THREE

٣٣- فَضْلُ مُعَاذِ بْنِ جَبَلٍ رَضِيَ اللهُ عَنْهُ: أَخْرَجَ ابْنُ أَبِي شَيْبَةَ عَنِ ابْنِ مَسْعُودٍ رَضِيَ اللهُ عَنْهُ قَالَ: جَاءَ مُعَاذٌ إِلَى النَّبِيِّ صَلَّى اللهُ عَلَيْهِ وَسَلَّمَ فَقَالَ: يَا رَسُولَ اللهِ أَقْرِئْنِي, فَقَالَ رَسُولُ اللهِ صَلَّى اللهُ عَلَيْهِ وَسَلَّمَ: «أَقْرِئْهُ», فَأَقْرَأْتُهُ مَا كَانَ مَعِي, ثُمَّ اخْتَلَفْتُ أَنَا وَهُوَ إِلَى رَسُولِ اللهِ صَلَّى اللهُ عَلَيْهِ وَسَلَّمَ فَقَرَأَ مِنْهُ مُعَاذٌ, وَكَانَ مُعَلِّمًا مِنَ المُعَلِّمِينَ عَلَى عَهْدِ رَسُولِ اللهِ صَلَّى اللهُ عَلَيْهِ وَسَلَّمَ (٥٦).

وَأَخْرَجَ ابْنُ سَعْدٍ بِسَنَدٍ فِيهِ الوَاقِدِيُّ عَنْ كَعْبِ بْنِ مَالِكٍ رَضِيَ اللهُ عَنْهُ قَالَ: كَانَ مُعَاذُ بْنُ جَبَلٍ يُفْتِي النَّاسَ بِالمَدِينَةِ فِي حَيَاةِ النَّبِيِّ صَلَّى اللهُ عَلَيْهِ وَسَلَّمَ وَأَبِي بَكْرٍ (٥٧).

On the virtues of Muʿath ibn Jabal (may Allah be pleased with him, and may He grant him contentment), ibn Abi Shayba narrates that ibn Masʿud (may Allah be pleased with him, and may He grant him contentment) said, "Muʿath ibn Jabal once came to the Prophet (may Allah bless him, and may He grant him peace) and said to him, 'Oh Messenger of Allah! Teach me the Qur'an.' So the Messenger commanded me, 'Teach him.' So I recited to him and taught him all that I memorized myself. Some time later, he gained such proficiency in the Qur'an that he and I had a disagreement (concerning the Qur'an) that we were forced to settle in the

---

(٥٦) أخرجه ابن أبي شيبة في مصنفه (٧/١٧٣).

(٥٧) ذكره المتقي الهندي في كنز العمال (٧/٢٥١).

presence of the Messenger of Allah (may Allah bless him, and may He grant him peace). Indeed, he was a skilled teacher among the instructors of the Qur'an during the life of the Messenger of Allah (may Allah bless him, and may He grant him peace)." Ibn Sa'd also records another narration quoting Ka'b ibn Malik (may Allah be pleased with him, and may He grant him contentment). It should be known that this latter hadith's chain of narrators contains al-Waqidi,[58] who quotes Ka'b ibn Malik (may Allah bless him, and may He grant him peace) as having said, "It was the case that Mu'ath ibn Jabal used to provide legal verdicts for the people in al-Madina during the life of the Prophet (may Allah bless him, and may He grant him peace) and the life of Abu Bakr (may Allah be pleased with him, and may He grant him contentment)."

---

(58) The author mentions that the hadith's chain of narrators contains al-Waqidi out of academic integrity, because al-Waqidi is surrounded by a great deal of controversy concerning his fitness and skill in narrating hadith; most scholars have stated that he is not trustworthy while noting that he was not a proper narrator of prophetic traditions, but, rather a scholar of history. Nonetheless, some scholars gave him a seal of approval and regarded his narrations to be authentic.

HADITH THIRTY-FOUR

٣٤- فَضْلُ أَبِي أَيُّوبَ الأَنْصَارِيِّ رَضِيَ اللهُ عَنْهُ: أَخْرَجَ الرُّوْيَانِيُّ وَابْنُ عَسَاكِرَ عَنْ حَبِيبِ بْنِ أَبِي ثَابِتٍ أَنَّ أَبَا أَيُّوبَ نَزَلَ عَلَى ابْنِ عَبَّاسٍ فِي البَصْرَةِ فَفَرَّغَ لَهُ بَيْتَهُ، وَقَالَ: لَأَصْنَعَنَّ بِكَ كَمَا صَنَعْتَ بِرَسُولِ اللهِ صَلَّى اللهُ عَلَيْهِ وَسَلَّمَ، فَأَمَرَ أَهْلَهُ فَخَرَجُوا، وَقَالَ: لَكَ مَا فِي البَيْتِ كُلِّهِ، وَأَعْطَاهُ أَرْبَعِينَ أَلْفاً وَعِشْرِينَ مَمْلُوكاً (٥٩).

Concerning the stature of Abu Ayyub al-Ansari (may Allah be pleased with him, and may He grant him contentment), ar-Rawyani and ibn 'Asakir narrate that Habib ibn Abi Thabit said, "Abu Ayyub once went to visit ibn 'Abbas in al-Basra. The entire household of ibn 'Abbas was surprised at his arrival. Ibn 'Abbas then said, 'I swear by Allah, I will make my house yours just you made yours the Messenger of Allah's when you hosted him.' Ibn 'Abbas (may Allah be pleased wit him, and may He grant him contentment) then ordered his family to leave the house telling Abu Ayyub, 'Everything in the house is yours!' He then gave him 40,020 slaves."[60]

---

(٥٩) أخرجه ابن عساكر في تاريخ دمشق (٥٥/١٦).

(60) Translator's note: 'Abdullah ibn 'Abbas (may Allah be pleased with him, and may He grant him contentment) was at that time the governor of Basra, which was a city under the caliphate and authority of Imam 'Ali (may Allah be pleased with him, and may He grant him contentment).

HADITH THIRTY-FIVE

٣٥- فَضْلُ أُبَيِّ بْنِ كَعْبٍ رَضِيَ اللهُ عَنْهُ: أَخْرَجَ الطَّبَرَانِيُّ فِي الأَوْسَطِ وَابْنُ عَسَاكِرَ عَنْ أُبَيِّ بْنِ كَعْبٍ رَضِيَ اللهُ عَنْهُ قَالَ: قَالَ لِي رَسُوْلُ اللهِ صَلَّى اللهُ عَلَيْهِ وَسَلَّمَ: «يَا أَبَا المُنْذِرِ إِنِّي أُمِرْتُ أَنْ أَعْرِضَ عَلَيْكَ القُرْآنَ» قُلْتُ: يَا رَسُوْلَ اللهِ, بِاللهِ آمَنْتُ, وَعَلَى يَدَيْكَ أَسْلَمْتُ, وَمِنْكَ تَعَلَّمْتُ, فَرَدَّ النَّبِيُّ صَلَّى اللهُ عَلَيْهِ وَسَلَّمَ القَوْلَ, قُلْتُ: يَا رَسُوْلَ اللهِ وَذُكِرْتُ هُنَالِكَ ؟ قَالَ: «نَعَمْ بِاسْمِكَ وَنَسَبِكَ فِي المَلَإِ الأَعْلَى» قَالَ: فَاقْرَأْ إِذًا يَا رَسُوْلَ اللهِ (٦١).

On the excellence of Ubayy ibn Kaʿb (may Allah be pleased with him, and may He grant him contentment), at-Tabarani and ibn 'Asakir narrate that Ubayy ibn Kaʿb himself said, "Allah's Emissary (may Allah bless him, and may He grant him peace) said to me, 'Oh Abu Munthir! I have been commanded to present the Qur'an to you.' I responded, 'Oh Emissary of Allah! I swear by Allah that I have believed, that I have accepted Islam at your hands and that I only learn from you.' The Prophet (may Allah bless him, and may He grant him peace) then repeated his initial statement, after which, I said, 'Oh Emissary of Allah! Was I named specifically in this command?' 'Yes, by name and by your assignment in the heavens above,' the Prophet (may Allah bless him, and may He grant him peace) said. I then responded, 'Then recite to me and teach me, oh Emissary of Allah.'"

---

(٦١) أخرجه الطبراني في الأوسط (٤٥٥).

HADITH THIRTY-SIX

٣٦- فَضْلُ حُذَيْفَةَ بْنِ اليَمَانِ رَضِيَ اللهُ عَنْهُ: أَخْرَجَ ابْنُ عَسَاكِرَ عَنْ حُذَيْفَةَ بْنِ اليَمَانِ رَضِيَ اللهُ عَنْهُمَا قَالَ: بَعَثَنِي رَسُولُ اللهِ صَلَّى اللهُ عَلَيْهِ وَسَلَّمَ سَرِيَّةً وَحْدِي(٦٢), وَكَانَ حُذَيْفَةُ صَاحِبَ سِرِّ رَسُولِ اللهِ صَلَّى اللهُ عَلَيْهِ وَسَلَّمَ فِي المُنَافِقِينَ.

رَوَى رُسْتَةُ عَنْ زَيْدِ بْنِ وَهْبٍ قَالَ: مَاتَ رَجُلٌ مِنَ المُنَافِقِينَ فَلَمْ يُصَلِّ عَلَيْهِ حُذَيْفَةُ, فَقَالَ لَهُ عُمَرُ: أَمِنَ القَوْمِ هَذَا ؟ قَالَ: نَعَمْ, قَالَ: بِاللهِ أَمِنْهُمْ أَنَا ؟ قَالَ: لَا, وَلَنْ أُخْبِرَ بِهِ بَعْدَكَ أَحَداً(٦٣).

Concerning the stature of the companion Huthayfa ibn al-Yaman (may Allah be pleased with him, and may He grant him contentment), ibn 'Asakir quotes Huthayfa himself as saying, "The Messenger of Allah (may Allah bless him, and may He grant him peace) dispatched me to tackle an entire endeavor by myself." As it was known, Huthayfa attached himself to the Prophet (may Allah bless him, and may He grant him peace) and learned many secrets from him concerning the hypocrites. Rista narrated that Zayd ibn Wahb said, "It happened that a man – who was later revealed to be a hypocrite – had died. Huthayfa did not participate in his funeral prayer, and due to this, 'Umar asked him, 'Was this man one of the hypocrites?' 'Yes,' Huthayfa answered.

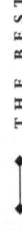

---

(٦٢) ذكره المتقي الهندي في كنز العمال (٣٤٥/١٣).

(٦٣) ذكره المتقي الهندي في كنز العمال (١٤٩/٧).

'Am I included among them?' 'Umar asked. 'No, and after you, I will not inform anyone of his status ever again,' Huthayfa (may Allah be pleased with him, and may He grant him contentment) said."

HADITH THIRTY-SEVEN

٣٧- فَضْلُ أُسَيْدِ بْنِ حُضَيْرٍ رضي اللهُ عَنْهُ: أَخْرَجَ الطَّبَرَانِيُّ وَغَيْرُهُ عَنْ أُسَيْدِ بْنِ حُضَيْرٍ قَالَ: كُنْتُ أُصَلِّي فِي لَيْلَةٍ مُقْمِرَةٍ وَقَدْ وَثَبَتْ فَرَسِي فَجَالَتْ جَوْلَةً فَفَزِعْتُ, ثُمَّ جَالَتْ أُخْرَى فَرَفَعْتُ رَأْسِي وَإِذَا ظُلَّةٌ غَشِيَتْنِي وَإِذَا هِيَ قَدْ حَالَتْ بَيْنِي وَبَيْنَ القَمَرِ, فَفَزِعْتُ فَدَخَلْتُ البَيْتَ, فَلَمَّا أَصْبَحْتُ ذَكَرْتُ ذَلِكَ لِلنَّبِيِّ صَلَّى اللهُ عَلَيْهِ وَسَلَّمَ فَقَالَ: «تِلْكَ المَلَائِكَةُ جَاءَتْ تَسْتَمِعُ قِرَاءَتَكَ مِنْ آخِرِ اللَّيْلِ سُورَةَ البَقَرَةِ».⁽⁶⁴⁾

Concerning the virtue of Asyad ibn Haydar (may Allah be pleased with him, and may He grant him contentment), at-Tabarani and others narrated that Asyad ibn Haydar himself said, "I was once praying on a moonlit night when my horse got up and began a slow gallop around me; I became frightened. (I resumed reciting), but, then, again, my horse became unsettled, so I looked up and there was cloud of lights descending upon me to the point of coming between me and the full moon. I was very much terrified, so I fled into the house. Upon waking up the next morning, I mentioned what happened to the Prophet (may Allah bless him, and may He grant him peace). He informed me, 'Those were angels descending to listen to your recitation of the Qur'an from Surah al-Layl and Surah al-Baqara.'"

---

(٦٤) أخرجه الطبراني في الأوسط (٦٧٣٥).

HADITH THIRTY-EIGHT

٣٨- فَضْلُ سَلْمَانَ الفَارِسِيِّ رَضِيَ اللهُ عَنْهُ: أَخْرَجَ عَبْدُ الرَّزَّاقِ عَنْ سَلْمَانَ الفَارِسِيِّ رَضِيَ اللهُ عَنْهُ فِي حَدِيثٍ طَوِيلٍ أَنَّهُ صَحِبَ رَاهِباً قَالَ لَهُ: إِنَّ اللهَ لَمْ يُعْطِ العَرَبَ مِنَ الأَنْبِيَاءِ أَحَداً, وَإِنَّهُ سَيَخْرُجُ مِنْهُمْ نَبِيٌّ, فَإِنْ أَدْرَكْتَهُ فَصَدِّقْهُ وَآمِنْ بِهِ, وَإِنَّ آيَتَهُ أَنْ يَقْبَلَ الهَدِيَّةَ وَلَا يَأْكُلَ الصَّدَقَةَ, وَإِنَّ فِي ظَهْرِهِ خَاتَمَ النُّبُوَّةِ, فَمَكَثْتُ مَا مَكَثْتُ, ثُمَّ قَالُوا: جَاءَ النَّبِيُّ صَلَّى اللهُ عَلَيْهِ وَسَلَّمَ إِلَى المَدِينَةِ, فَخَرَجْتُ مَعِي بِتَمْرٍ فَجِئْتُ إِلَيْهِ بِهِ, فَقَالَ: «مَا هَذَا؟» قُلْتُ: صَدَقَةٌ, قَالَ: لَا نَأْكُلُ الصَّدَقَةَ, فَأَخَذْتُهُ ثُمَّ أَتَيْتُهُ بِتَمْرٍ فَوَضَعْتُهُ بَيْنَ يَدَيْهِ فَقَالَ: «مَا هَذَا؟» قُلْتُ: هَدِيَّةٌ, فَأَكَلَ وَأَكَلَ مَنْ كَانَ عِنْدَهُ, ثُمَّ قُمْتُ وَرَاءَ ظَهْرِهِ لِأَنْظُرَ إِلَى الخَاتَمِ, فَفَطِنَ بِي فَأَلْقَى رِدَاءَهُ عَنْ مَنْكِبَيْهِ فَأَبْصَرْتُهُ, فَآمَنْتُ بِهِ وَصَدَّقْتُهُ, فَكَاتَبْتُ عَلَى مِائَةِ نَخْلَةٍ فَغَرَسَهَا رَسُولُ اللهِ صَلَّى اللهُ عَلَيْهِ وَسَلَّمَ بِيَدِهِ فَلَمْ يَحُلِ الحَوْلُ حَتَّى بَلَغَتْ وَأَكَلَ مِنْهَا^(٦٥).

On the excellence of Salman al-Farisi (may Allah be pleased with him, and may He grant him contentment), 'Abdurrazzaq presents a long narration that quotes Salman al-Farisi himself as describing his time living under the tutelage of a monk, who said to him, "Allah has not yet sent a prophet to the Arabs, but this will soon change as there is a prophet who will come forth from them. If you live to hear about him, then believe in him and follow him. He is a man, who if he is brought a gift, he accepts it, but he does not accept or eat from charity. Further, on his back,

---

(٦٥) أخرجه عبد الرزاق في مصنفه (٤٢٠/٨).

he has the seal of prophecy. I remained in those lands for sometime until I heard the people talking of a man claiming prophethood in al-Madina. So I set out with a portion of dates to deliver it to him (and test him). I presented it to him on my arrival, at which he asked me, 'What is this?' I said, 'Charity.' He said, 'We do not eat from charity.' So I picked up the dates, and I came before him a second time and presented him the dates, and he again asked me, 'What is this?' I responded, 'A gift,' upon which he accepted it and he ate from it inviting those in his company to eat from it also. I then stood up to make an attempt to look behind his back to spot the seal of prophecy. He immediately figured what I was attempting to do, and he threw his cloak from his shoulders. Upon seeing it, I believed in him immediately. I then took a contract for my freedom with the condition that I plant 100 date palm trees; the Messenger of Allah assisted me in planting these seeds with his very own hands, and a year did not pass before these trees bore fruit and the people ate from it."

HADITH THIRTY-NINE

٣٩- فَضْلُ مُعَاوِيَةَ رَضِيَ اللهُ عَنْهُ: أَخْرَجَ التِّرْمِذِيُّ عَنْ عَبْدِ الرَّحْمَنِ بْنِ أَبِي عُمَيْرَةَ عَنِ النَّبِيِّ صَلَّى اللهُ عَلَيْهِ وَسَلَّمَ أَنَّهُ قَالَ لِمُعَاوِيَةَ: «اللَّهُمَّ اجْعَلْهُ هَادِياً مَهْدِياً وَاهْدِ بِهِ».^(٦٦)

On the merit of Mu'awiya (may Allah be pleased with him, and may He grant him contentment), at-Tirmithi narrates that 'Abdurrahman ibn Abi 'Umayra reported that the Prophet (may Allah bless him, and may He grant him peace) said concerning Mu'awiya, "Oh Allah! Guide him, make him a guide for others and bring forth Your guidance through him."

---

(٦٦) أخرجه الترمذي (٤٢١٣).

HADITH FORTY

٤٠- فَضْلُ عَمْرِو بْنِ العَاصِ رَضِيَ اللهُ عَنْهُ: أَخْرَجَ التِّرْمِذِيُّ عَنْ عُقْبَةَ بْنِ عَامِرٍ رَضِيَ اللهُ عَنْهُ قَالَ: قَالَ رَسُولُ اللهِ صَلَّى اللهُ عَلَيْهِ وَسَلَّمَ: «أَسْلَمَ النَّاسُ وَآمَنَ عَمْرُو بْنُ العَاصِ». ⁽⁶⁷⁾

On the merit of 'Amr ibn al-'As (may Allah be pleased with him, and may He grant him contentment), at-Tirmithi records for us that 'Uqba ibn 'Amir (may Allah be pleased with him, and may He grant him contentment) said, "The Messenger of Allah said, 'At the time when the people simply accepted Islam, 'Amr went beyond that and believed immediately.'"

(٦٧) أخرجه الترمذي (٣٨٤٤).

خَاتِمَةٌ فِي فَضْلِ الصَّحَابَةِ مُطْلَقاً

CONCLUSION

ON THE VIRTUES OF THE COMPANIONS
ALTOGETHER AS A CLASS BY THEMSELVES

عَنْ أَبِي سَعِيدٍ الْخُدْرِيِّ رَضِيَ اللهُ عَنْهُ عَنْ رَسُولِ اللهِ صَلَّى اللهُ عَلَيْهِ وَسَلَّمَ قَالَ: «لَا تَسُبُّوا أَصْحَابِي؛ فَلَوْ أَنَّ أَحَدَكُمْ أَنْفَقَ مِثْلَ أُحُدٍ ذَهَبًا مَا بَلَغَ مُدَّ أَحَدِهِمْ وَلَا نَصِيفَهُ». (٦٨) رَوَاهُ الشَّيْخَانِ.

On the authority of Abu Saʿid al-Khudri, who reported that the Messenger of Allah (may Allah bless him, and may He grant him peace) said, "Do not insult my companions! It is the case that even if any of you were to give gold as charity in equivalence to the weight of Mount Uhud, you would not reach the stature that my companions have reached nor would you secure a reward like that which awaits them in the hereafter." Narrated by the two Shaykhs.

---

(٦٨) أخرجه البخاري (٣٦٧٣) ومسلم (٦٦٥١).

وَعَنْ أَبِي مُوسَى الْأَشْعَرِيِّ رَضِيَ اللهُ عَنْهُ قَالَ: رَفَعَ -يَعْنِي: النَّبِيَّ صَلَّى اللهُ عَلَيْهِ وَسَلَّمَ- رَأْسَهُ إِلَى السَّمَاءِ فَقَالَ: «النُّجُومُ أَمَنَةٌ لِلسَّمَاءِ، فَإِذَا ذَهَبَتِ النُّجُومُ أَتَى السَّمَاءَ مَا تُوعَدُ، وَأَنَا أَمَنَةٌ لِأَصْحَابِي، فَإِذَا ذَهَبْتُ أَتَى أَصْحَابِي مَا يُوعَدُونَ، وَأَصْحَابِي أَمَنَةٌ لِأُمَّتِي، فَإِذَا ذَهَبَ أَصْحَابِي أَتَى أُمَّتِي مَا يُوعَدُونَ». (٦٩) رَوَاهُ مُسْلِمٌ.

On the authority of Abu Musa al-Ash'ari (may Allah be pleased with him, and may He grant him contentment), who reported that the Prophet (may Allah bless him, and may He grant him peace) once looked towards the heavens and said, "The stars are a reassuring factor for the sky, so when the stars disappear, the sky will be me met with what it has been promised.[70] In a similar fashion, I am reassurance for my companions, so when I leave my companions will be presented with what they were promised. Finally, and by extension, my companions are a securing factor for my nation, so when they pass on, my nation will be given what it was promised."

---

(٦٩) أخرجه مسلم (٢٥٣١).

(70) The Prophet (may Allah bless him, and may He grant him peace) is making reference here to the events that will occur on the Day of Judgment.

وَعَنْ عِمْرَانَ بْنِ حُصَيْنٍ رَضِيَ اللهُ عَنْهُمَا قَالَ: قَالَ رَسُولُ اللهِ صَلَّى اللهُ عَلَيْهِ وَسَلَّمَ: «خَيْرُ أُمَّتِي قَرْنِي، ثُمَّ الَّذِينَ يَلُونَهُمْ، ثُمَّ الَّذِينَ يَلُونَهُمْ، ثُمَّ إِنَّ بَعْدَهُمْ قَوْمًا يَشْهَدُونَ وَلَا يُسْتَشْهَدُونَ، وَيَخُونُونَ وَلَا يُؤْتَمَنُونَ، وَيَنْذُرُونَ وَلَا يَفُونَ، وَيَظْهَرُ فِيهِمُ السِّمَنُ». وَفِي رِوَايَةٍ: «وَيَحْلِفُونَ وَلَا يُسْتَحْلَفُونَ». رَوَاهُ الشَّيْخَانِ. (٧١)

The two Shaykhs both narrate that 'Imran ibn Husayn (may Allah be pleased with him, and may He grant him contentment) said that the Messenger of Allah (may Allah bless him, and may He grant him peace) said, "The best of my nation are those who are from my generation,[72] and then – after them in stature – are those who come after them and after them is the generation who will come after the second generation. Thereafter, there will come a people who will bear witness without be called to witness; they will betray and they will be far removed from trustworthiness; they will make promises but not fulfill them. Among their signs will be obesity." In another narration the Prophet (may Allah bless him, and may He grant him peace) says, "They will swear by Allah concerning legal matters without being asked to swear."

---

(٧١) أخرجه البخاري (٢٥٠٨) ومسلم (٢٥٣٥).

(72) The Prophet (may Allah bless him, and may He grant him peace) intends his companions here.

وَعَنْ عُمَرَ رَضِيَ اللهُ عَنْهُ قَالَ: قَالَ رَسُولُ اللهِ صَلَّى اللهُ عَلَيْهِ وَسَلَّمَ: «أَكْرِمُوا أَصْحَابِي، فَإِنَّهُمْ خِيَارُكُمْ، ثُمَّ الَّذِينَ يَلُونَهُمْ، ثُمَّ الَّذِينَ يَلُونَهُمْ، ثُمَّ يَظْهَرُ الكَذِبُ حَتَّى إِنَّ الرَّجُلَ لَيَحْلِفُ وَلَا يُسْتَحْلَفُ، وَيَشْهَدُ وَلَا يُسْتَشْهَدُ، أَلَا مَنْ سَرَّهُ بُحْبُوحَةُ الجَنَّةِ فَلْيَلْزَمِ الجَمَاعَةَ، فَإِنَّ الشَّيْطَانَ مَعَ الفَذِّ وَهُوَ مِنَ الِاثْنَيْنِ أَبْعَدُ، وَلَا يَخْلُوَنَّ رَجُلٌ بِامْرَأَةٍ؛ فَإِنَّ الشَّيْطَانَ ثَالِثُهُمْ، وَمَنْ سَرَّتْهُ حَسَنَتُهُ وَسَاءَتْهُ سَيِّئَتُهُ فَهُوَ مُؤْمِنٌ». (٧٣) رَوَاهُ النَّسَائِيُّ.

On the authority of 'Umar (may Allah be pleased with him, and may He grant him contentment), who said, "The Messenger of Allah (may Allah bless him, and may He grant him peace) said, 'Honor my companions; indeed, they are the best of you. The best after them will be the generation that follows them, and then the generation after that second generation. Thereafter, dishonesty will become a societal norm, so much so that a man will swear on sensitive legal matters using Allah's name without even being asked to swear. Similarly, a man will bear witness without being called to bear witness. So whoever of you is looking forward to the next life in paradise, then let him not stray from the main body of the Muslims; indeed, Satan preys upon the loner; it is the case that when two believers come together he (Satan) is forced to keep a further distance. Do not sit with any woman in isolation; indeed, (if they do so) the third among them will be Satan. Whoever is gladdened by his good deeds – but is distressed by his evil deeds – is a believer.'"

---

(٧٣) أخرجه الترمذي (٢١٦٥)، والنسائي في الكبرى (٩٢٢٥).

وَعَنْ جَابِرٍ رَضِيَ اللهُ عَنْهُ عَنِ النَّبِيِّ صَلَّى اللهُ عَلَيْهِ وَسَلَّمَ قَالَ: «لَا تَمَسُّ النَّارُ مُسْلِمًا رَآنِيْ أَوْ رَأَى مَنْ رَآنِيْ»(٧٤). رَوَاهُ التِّرْمِذِيُّ.

Jabir (may Allah be pleased with him, and may He grant him contentment) said, "The fire will not touch any Muslim who has seen me or has seen someone who saw me." Narrated by at-Tirmithi.

---

(٧٤) أخرجه الترمذي (٣٨٥٨).

وَعَنْ عَبْدِ اللهِ بْنِ مُغَفَّلٍ رَضِيَ اللهُ عَنْهُ قَالَ: قَالَ رَسُولُ اللهِ صَلَّى اللهُ عَلَيْهِ وَسَلَّمَ: «اللَّهَ اللَّهَ فِي أَصْحَابِي، اللَّهَ اللَّهَ فِي أَصْحَابِي، لَا تَتَّخِذُوهُمْ غَرَضًا مِنْ بَعْدِي، فَمَنْ أَحَبَّهُمْ فَبِحُبِّي أَحَبَّهُمْ، وَمَنْ أَبْغَضَهُمْ فَبِبُغْضِي أَبْغَضَهُمْ، وَمَنْ آذَاهُمْ فَقَدْ آذَانِي، وَمَنْ آذَانِي فَقَدْ آذَى اللَّهَ، وَمَنْ آذَى اللَّهَ فَيُوشِكُ أَنْ يَأْخُذَهُ»^(٧٥). رَوَاهُ التِّرْمِذِيُّ.

Abdullah ibn Mughaffal (may Allah be pleased with him, and may He grant him contentment) reported that the Messenger of Allah (may Allah bless him, and may He grant him peace) said, "Allah! Allah! Be conscious of Allah, as it concerns my companions, fear Allah! Do not treat them with the slightest disrespect or contempt when I am no longer present. Whoever honors and shows love to my companions, then they have attained my love; conversely, whoever resents them, then upon them lies my resentment. Whoever insults them, then they have indeed insulted me, and whoever insults me has indeed insulted Allah Almighty; whoever insults Allah is on the verge of Allah smiting him and taking him to task." Narrated by at-Tirmithi.

---

(٧٥) أخرجه الترمذي (٣٨٦٢).

وَعَنْ أَنَسٍ رَضِيَ اللهُ عَنْهُ قَالَ: قَالَ رَسُولُ اللهِ صَلَّى اللهُ عَلَيْهِ وَسَلَّمَ: «مَثَلُ أَصْحَابِي فِي أُمَّتِي كَالْمِلْحِ فِي الطَّعَامِ، لَا يَصْلُحُ الطَّعَامُ إِلَّا بِالْمِلْحِ»(٧٦).

قَالَ الحَسَنُ البَصْرِيُّ: فَقَدْ ذَهَبَ مِلْحُنَا فَكَيْفَ نَصْلُحُ؟ رَوَاهُ البَغَوِيُّ فِي شَرْحِ السُّنَّةِ.

Anas ibn Malik (may Allah be pleased with him, and may He grant him contentment) reported that the Messenger of Allah (may Allah bless him, and may He grant him peace) said, "The relation of my companions to my nation is similar to that of salt to any form of cuisine; no meal can be considered proper without the addition of salt." Al-Hasan al-Basri (may Allah be pleased with him, and may He grant him contentment) is reported to have commented on this hadith, "The fact is our salt has gone, so how can we become upright?" This quote from al-Hasan was taken from al-Baghawi's commentary on *as-Sunnah*.

---

(٧٦) أخرجه الطبراني في الكبير (٦٩٥٤).

وَعَنْ عَبْدِ اللهِ بْنِ بُرَيْدَةَ عَنْ أَبِيهِ رَضِيَ اللهُ عَنْهُ قَالَ: قَالَ رَسُولُ اللهِ صَلَّى اللهُ عَلَيْهِ وَسَلَّمَ: «مَا مِنْ أَحَدٍ مِنْ أَصْحَابِي يَمُوتُ بِأَرْضٍ إِلَّا بُعِثَ قَائِدًا وَنُورًا لَهُمْ يَوْمَ الْقِيَامَةِ». [77] رَوَاهُ التِّرْمِذِيُّ.

'Abdullah ibn Burayda (may Allah be pleased with him, and may He grant him contentment) reported that the Messenger of Allah (may Allah bless him, and may He grant him peace) said, "None of my companions die in any place except that they will come forth from that place on the Day of Judgment as standard bearers of light." Narrated by at-Tirmithi.

---

(77) أخرجه الترمذي (3865).

عَنِ ابْنِ عُمَرَ رَضِيَ اللهُ عَنْهُ قَالَ: قَالَ رَسُولُ اللهِ صَلَّى اللهُ عَلَيْهِ وَسَلَّمَ: «إِذَا رَأَيْتُمُ الَّذِي يَسُبُّونَ أَصْحَابِي فَقُولُوا: لَعْنَةُ اللَّهِ عَلَى شَرِّكُمْ»(٧٨). رَوَاهُ التِّرْمِذِيُّ.

'Umar ibn al-Khattab (may Allah be pleased with him, and may He grant him contentment) said that the Messenger of Allah (may Allah bless him, and may He grant him peace) said, "When you see the people cursing my companions, say to them, 'May the curse of Allah be upon this evil that you have concocted.'" Narrated by at-Tirmithi.

---

(٧٨) أخرجه الترمذي (٣٨٦٦).

وَعَنْ عُمَرَ رَضِيَ اللهُ عَنْهُ قَالَ: سَمِعْتُ رَسُوْلَ اللهِ صَلَّى اللهُ عَلَيْهِ وَسَلَّمَ يَقُوْلُ: «سَأَلْتُ رَبِّي عَنِ اخْتِلَافِ أَصْحَابِيْ مِنْ بَعْدِيْ، فَأَوْحَى إِلَيَّ: يَا مُحَمَّدُ إِنَّ أَصْحَابَكَ عِنْدِيْ بِمَنْزِلَةِ النُّجُوْمِ فِي السَّمَاءِ، بَعْضُهَا أَضْوَأُ مِنْ بَعْضٍ، وَلِكُلٍّ نُوْرٌ، فَمَنْ أَخَذَ بِشَيْءٍ مِمَّا هُمْ عَلَيْهِ مِنِ اخْتِلَافِهِمْ فَهُوَ عِنْدِيْ عَلَى هُدَى». قَالَ: وَقَالَ رَسُوْلُ اللهِ صَلَّى اللهُ عَلَيْهِ وَسَلَّمَ: «أَصْحَابِيْ كَالنُّجُوْمِ، فَبِأَيِّهِمُ اقْتَدَيْتُمُ اهْتَدَيْتُمْ»(٧٩). رَوَاهُمَا رَزِيْنٌ.

'Umar (may Allah be pleased with him, and may He grant him contentment) also said, "I heard the Messenger of Allah (may Allah bless him, and may He grant him peace) say, 'I asked my Lord about the differences that will occur between my companions after I pass on, and He then revealed to me, "Oh Muhammad! Your companions, in My regard, are like the stars in the sky; some of them are more luminous than others, yet all of them are sources of light. So whoever follows something that he has proof for from you – despite their differences – I am satisfied with them as being upon guidance." 'Umar (may Allah be pleased with him, and may He grant him contentment) also reported that the Prophet (may Allah bless him, and may He grant him peace) said, "My companions are similar to the stars; if you follow anyone of them, you will be guided." Both of these narrations were recorded by Ruzayn.[80]

(٧٩) أخرجه ابن بطة في الإبانة الكبرى (٢/٢٢٠).

(80) Translator's note: The two narrations here maybe questionable in their authenticity. The editor of the Arabic text cites a different source for these two narrations; he cites *al-Ibana al-Kubra*, which was compiled by ibn Batta, who –

وَاعْلَمْ أَنَّ فَضَائِلَ أَصْحَابِ رَسُولِ اللهِ صَلَّى اللَّهُ عَلَيْهِ وَسَلَّمَ كَثِيرَةٌ جِدًّا، وَحَسْبُكَ أَنَّهُمْ هُمُ الْمُبَلِّغُونَ دِينَ الْإِسْلَامِ وَسَائِرَ مَا يَتَفَرَّعُ عَنْهُ مِنَ الْأَحْكَامِ إِلَى مَنْ بَعْدَهُمْ، فَلَهُمْ أَجْرُهُمْ وَأَجْرُ كُلِّ مَنْ عَمِلَ بِمَا بَلَّغُوهُ مِنَ الدِّينِ إِلَى يَوْمِ الْقِيَامَةِ؛ لِقَوْلِهِ صَلَّى اللَّهُ عَلَيْهِ وَسَلَّمَ: «مَنْ سَنَّ سُنَّةً حَسَنَةً فَلَهُ أَجْرُهَا وَأَجْرُ مَنْ عَمِلَ بِهَا إِلَى يَوْمِ الْقِيَامَةِ».^(٨١)

Know, dear reader, that the virtues and merits of the companions are abounding and innumerable; sufficient enough is that it is through their sacrifice and dedication that this religion spread – without even delving into the the successive benefits and varying rulings which arose from – and grew directly out of – of their transmission of the religion. Indeed, they have written for them the recompense directly tied with their own actions in addition to the reward of their students and the reward of all those successive, latter generations yet to come until the Day of Judgment. This is indicated by the Prophet (may Allah bless him, and may He grant him peace) saying, "Whoever establishes a righteous norm among the people will have the reward of all those who follow him in that action until the Day of Judgment."

---

although he was a righteous scholar and a man of asceticism - was nonetheless a controversial figure concerning his narration of hadith. The translator mentions this here out of academic integrity, but, of course, Allah knows better concerning the reality of such affairs. For further reading see the entry on ibn Batta in the Arabic text *Lisan al-Mizan*, by ibn Hajr al-'Asqalani.

(٨١) أخرجه الطبراني في مسند الشاميين (٢٥٦٠).

وَرَوَى مُسْلِمٌ عَنْ أَبِي مَسْعُودٍ البَدْرِيّ رَضِيَ اللهُ عَنْهُ قَالَ: قَالَ رَسُولُ اللهِ صَلَّى اللهُ عَلَيْهِ وَسَلَّمَ: «مَنْ دَلَّ عَلَى خَيْرٍ فَلَهُ مِثْلُ أَجْرِ فَاعِلِهِ». (٨٢)

Imam Muslim narrates that Abu Mas'ud al-Badri (may Allah be pleased with him, and may He grant him contentment) reported that the Messenger of Allah (may Allah bless him, and may He grant him peace) said, "He who guides to any specific good will have the reward of he who performs that good."

---

(٨٢) أخرجه مسلم (١٨٩٣).

وَرَوَى مُسْلِمٌ أَيْضاً عَنْ أَبِي هُرَيْرَةَ رَضِيَ اللهُ عَنْهُ أَنَّ رَسُولَ اللهِ صَلَّى اللهُ عَلَيْهِ وَسَلَّمَ قَالَ: «مَنْ دَعَا إِلَى هُدًى كَانَ لَهُ مِنَ الأَجْرِ مِثْلُ أُجُورِ مَنْ تَبِعَهُ، لَا يَنْقُصُ ذَلِكَ مِنْ أُجُورِهِمْ شَيْئًا، وَمَنْ دَعَا إِلَى ضَلَالَةٍ كَانَ عَلَيْهِ مِنَ الْإِثْمِ مِثْلُ آثَامِ مَنْ تَبِعَهُ لَا يَنْقُصُ ذَلِكَ مِنْ آثَامِهِمْ شَيْئًا».[83]

Imam Muslim also records for us that Abu Hurayra (may Allah be pleased with him, and may He grant him contentment) reported that the Messenger of Allah (may Allah bless him, and may He grant him contentment) said, "Whoever calls the people to guidance will have the rewards of all all those who follow him – without the rewards of any of them being reduced in any way, shape or form. Conversely, whoever calls the people to misguidance will be held accountable for his own deviance as well that of all of those follow him – without this reducing from any of their evil deeds in the least."

---

(83) أخرجه مسلم (2676).

وَأَمَّا مَا وَقَعَ بَيْنَهُمْ مِنَ الْحُرُوبِ وَالْخِلَافَاتِ الْمَبْنِيَّةِ كُلِّهَا عَلَى اجْتِهَادِهِمْ فِي طَلَبِ الْحَقِّ فَأَصَابَ بَعْضُهُمْ وَأَخْطَأَ البَعْضُ, فَإِنَّ لِلْمُخْطِئِ مِنْهُمْ أَجْراً عَلَى اجْتِهَادِهِ فِي طَلَبِ الْحَقِّ. وَمَا كَانَ بَيْنَهُمْ مِنَ العَوَارِضِ البَشَرِيَّةِ فَهَذِهِ يَغْفِرُهَا اللهُ لَهُمْ بِفَضْلِهِ إِنْ شَاءَ؛ كَرَامَةً لِحَبِيبِهِ الأَعْظَمِ صَلَّى اللهُ عَلَيْهِ وَسَلَّمَ. وَهُمْ أَوْلَى النَّاسِ فِي أَنْ يَكُونُوا مَظْهَراً لِقَوْلِهِ تَعَالَى: {وَنَزَعْنَا مَا فِي صُدُورِهِم مِّنْ غِلٍّ إِخْوَانًا عَلَىٰ سُرُرٍ مُّتَقَابِلِينَ}.

As it concerns the wars and differences of opinion which occurred between the companions, all of these affairs were rooted in each of their individual endeavors and struggles to arrive at the truth; some of them were correct in their conclusions – while others may have been mistaken. Indeed, it is the case that those who were mistaken in their search for the truth achieve one reward. Furthermore, the story of the companions is a human experience, something that Allah, if He wills, can forgive out of His infinite grace and out of honor for His Beloved Prophet (may Allah bless him, and may He grant him peace). The verse in the Qur'an is most applicable to them; as He says, "We will remove all rancor and resentment from their hearts; as brothers, they will recline facing each other upon elevated, lofty seats."[84]

---

(84) Surah al-Hijr, *ayah* 47.

فَأَسْأَلُ اللهَ العَظِيمَ رَبَّ العَرْشِ الكَرِيمَ أَنْ يُمِيتَنِي عَلَى حُبِّهِمْ أَجْمَعِينَ، وَحُبِّ جَمِيعِ أَهْلِ البَيْتِ الطَّيِّبِينَ الطَّاهِرِينَ، وَأَنْ تَكُونَ مَحَبَّتِي لَهُمْ كَثْرَةً وَقِلَّةً بِنِسْبَةِ دَرَجَاتِهِمْ فِي المَحَبَّةِ عِنْدَ الحَبِيبِ الأَعْظَمِ سَيِّدِنَا مُحَمَّدٍ سَيِّدِ المُرْسَلِينَ صَلَّى اللهُ عَلَيْهِ وَسَلَّمَ وَعَلَى آلِهِ وَصَحْبِهِ أَجْمَعِينَ، وَالحَمْدُ للهِ رَبِّ العَالَمِينَ.

I ask Allah, the Lord of Honorable Throne, to allow us to hold firm to and die in a state where we love all of them and all of the Prophet's family, those pure, fragrant souls. May Allah make my love for each of them proportional to their love for the Beloved Prophet, our master, Muhammad, the commander and leader of the prophets (may Allah bless him, and may He grant him peace) – and may He extend His blessings and peace upon his family and all of his companions. And all praise is due to Allah, the Lord of the worlds.

www.ingramcontent.com/pod-product-compliance
Lightning Source LLC
LaVergne TN
LVHW092056060526
838201LV00047B/1423